THE CLASSIC AMERICAN
QUILT COLLECTION®
⬥
LOG CABIN

Series Editor
Mary V. Green

Rodale Press, Emmaus, Pennsylvania

OUR PURPOSE

*"We inspire and enable people to improve
their lives and the world around them."*

Executive Editor: *Margaret Lydic Balitas*

Managing Editor and Series Development:
Suzanne Nelson

Senior Associate Editor: *Mary V. Green*

Technical Writer: *Janet Wickell*

Quilt Scout: *Bettina Havig*

Copy Editor: *Carolyn Mandarano*

Copy Manager: *Dolores Plikaitis*

Office Manager: *Karen Earl-Braymer*

Administrative Assistant: *Susan Nickol*

Art Director: *Michael Mandarano*

Cover and Interior Designer: *Denise Shade*

Book Layout: *Lisa Palmer*

Cover Photographer: *Mitch Mandel*

Interior Photographers: *John Hamel and Mitch Mandel*

Photo Stylist: *Marianne L. Laubach*

Illustrator: *Charles M. Metz*

Intern: *Tanya L. Lipinski*

If you have any questions or comments concerning this book, please write to:
Rodale Press, Inc.
Book Readers' Service
33 East Minor Street
Emmaus, PA 18098

Quotation on page v from *The Quilters: Women and Domestic Art,* by Patricia Cooper and Norma Bradley Allen. New York: Anchor Books/Doubleday, 1989.

The quilt shown on pages 128–129 is owned by Doris Adomsky of Ivyland, Penn.

Library of Congress Cataloging-in-Publication Data

The Classic American quilt collection. Log Cabin /
  Mary V. Green, series editor.
      p. cm.
    ISBN 0–87596–629–2 hardcover
    1. Patchwork—United States—Patterns. 2.
Quilting—United States—Patterns. 3. Log cabin
quilts—United States. I. Green, Mary V.
TT835.C58   1994
746.9'7—dc20   94–8403
                                                              CIP
Distributed in the book trade by St. Martin's Press
  6 8 10 9 7   hardcover

CONTENTS

ACKNOWLEDGMENTS

Sunshine and Shadow, made by Bettina Havig; owned by Joyce Gross, Petaluma, California. This quilt was a gift to Joyce from Bettina. Joyce is a known quilt collector, quilt historian, and, since 1973, publisher of *Quilter's Journal.* In 1993, she was honored by the American Museum of Quilts and Textiles in San Jose, California, with the exhibit "Portrait of a Quilter, Scholar, Author: Joyce Gross."

Scrap Half Log Cabin, made by Sharyn Craig, El Cajon, California. Sharyn is a nationally known quiltmaker, teacher, and author who enjoys challenging other quiltmakers to exercise their creativity. Her designs are based on traditional patterns, but she adds a subtle twist to create an original statement. Sharyn views her quiltmaking as a link to past and future generations and encourages all quilters to keep that current flowing.

Pineapple Log Cabin, owned by Edith Leeper, Columbia, Missouri. Edith bought this quilt in southeastern Missouri in the 1980s; unfortunately, its provenance is not known. Quilts have always been a part of Edith's life; her mother, grandmother, and great-grandmother were quiltmakers. Although not a quilter herself, Edith is a collector of quilts and quilt patterns and is the proud owner of a complete collection of the original Kansas City Star patterns published from 1928 through 1960.

Nineteenth-Century Amish Log Cabin, made by Elsie Schlabach, Millersburg, Ohio. Elsie was inspired to create a quilt in the tradition of Amish scrap quilts of the last century. The quilt uses 47 different colors and combines hand and machine piecing and hand quilting. Elsie has been quilting for about 14 years and has won numerous awards for her work. This quilt has won awards at the Quilter's Heritage in Lancaster, Pennsylvania, and the American Quilter's Society show in Paducah, Kentucky.

Paths to the Diamonds, made by Doris Heitman, Williamsburg, Iowa; quilted by Alice Williamson. Doris created her contemporary-looking quilt after hearing a lecture by quiltmaker and teacher Mary Ellen Hopkins. She likes Log Cabins because of the many variations possible. A longtime quiltmaker, Doris prefers wallhangings because she can finish them quickly and move on to the next project.

Barn Raising, made by Mark Stratton, Pasadena, California. Mark was introduced to quiltmaking by his mother, Carly Stratton, a former home-ec teacher who "let no one leave the house without learning to sew." He is inspired by images as diverse as traditional Amish quilts and the Navajo rugs he and his wife collect. This quilt is the result of what Mark calls "careful planning and consid-erable serendipity." Begun as a way to use up some teal fabric, it grew to include navy and royal blue, pink, purple, and magenta. It was hand quilted by an Amish family.

Courthouse Steps, pieced by Anne Fryer (born 1797); owned by the Randolph County Historical Society, Moberly, Missouri. This well-preserved nineteenth-century quilt was donated to the Historical Society by the family of Lucille and Willie Moler. It appears here courtesy of Bonnie Jacoby, an avid quilter and a member of the Historical Society.

Summer Night, made by Karen Stone, Dallas, Texas. Karen's quilt is actually reversible; the front and back are constructed simultaneously in a "flip-and-sew" technique taught by Emiko Toda Loeb. Karen began quilting in 1987 when she was expecting her first child. She quickly became hooked and now shares her enthusiasm through teaching.

Straight Furrows, owned by Woodin Wheel Antiques, Kalona, Iowa. The only thing known about this cheerful 1930s-era quilt is that it was made in Ottumwa, Iowa. The quilt appears here courtesy of Marilyn Woodin, the owner of Woodin Wheel Antiques and the Kalona Quilt and Textile Museum. Marilyn has been a quilt collector for 20 years, and she lectures on antique and Amish quilts.

Pineapple Variation, made by Terry Clothier Thompson, Lawrence, Kansas. Terry designed this quilt from memory after seeing a similar antique. Descended from a long line of quilters, Terry has been designing and making quilts herself since 1965. During that time, she has also taught classes, opened a quilt shop, marketed a line of quilt patterns, won awards, and seen her work in print in the publication *Best of Kansas Arts and Crafts.*

Logs Hexagonal, made by June Ryker, Lakewood, Colorado. June is a well-known quiltmaker, teacher, and author who has spent a great deal of time exploring and expanding the traditional Log Cabin. She has squeezed, stretched, and rounded the basic block into new and unique shapes. June has been quilting since 1973. Her patterns are published under the name The Quilted Lady.

Red, White, and Blue, probably made by Lillie A. Miller Rohrbach (born 1876); owned by Lucille Powell, Gilbertsville, Pennsylvania. This quilt is part of a collection of well-preserved quilts passed down in Lucille's family. Though it was definitely a family member, the actual quiltmaker's identity is uncertain. Lucille is not a quiltmaker herself, although she does have a deep appreciation for quilts. An elementary school art teacher, Lucille uses quilts to teach design concepts and tries to impress on her students the need to appreciate quilts as art.

INTRODUCTION

It just comes naturally, making a Log Cabin.
—Anonymous Texas Pioneer Settler

The romance of the Log Cabin lingers on some 125 years after American quilters first began piecing "logs" of fabric around a central square. It's not hard to imagine a pioneer woman on the frontier stitching together bits of fabric to impose some order and comfort on the chaos of her new life while her husband hewed logs to build a warm and safe homestead for his family. It's an appealing image steeped in Americana, the wife joining fabric strips in the same pattern her husband used to interlock the logs for their home.

While it's natural to assume that the first Log Cabin quilts originated on the American frontier, quilt historians cite traces of Log Cabin–type pieces found on Egyptian mummies and a very early English Log Cabin quilt that predates 1830. Although no one knows for certain how this design of overlapping strips originated, what we do know is that sometime during or right after the Civil War, during the 1860s and 1870s, American Log Cabin quilts began to appear. And they kept right on appearing as a Log Cabin craze swept the country, making the Log Cabin one of the most popular and widely made designs through the end of that century.

In a quiltmaking version of manifest destiny, American women took the pattern and made it truly their own, a reflection of the energies of a country growing by leaps and bounds. The pattern became identified with the pioneer spirit; a red center block came to symbolize the hearth of the home, and a yellow center represented a lantern placed in the window as a welcoming beacon. (During the Civil War, a Log Cabin quilt with black center squares hung on a clothesline was meant to signal a safe haven for the Underground Railroad.) In traditional Log Cabin blocks, one half is made of dark fabrics and the other of light fabrics. This continues the log home imagery even further, with the darks and lights in the quilt representing the shadows and firelight surrounding the hearth.

The names given to the different block settings reveal how closely this quilt was tied to a way of life in the nineteenth century. Barn Raising, Chimneys and Cornerstones, Straight Furrows, Sunshine and Shadow, and Courthouse Steps are just some of the hundreds of possible variations on this versatile block with its versatile settings. Log Cabin blocks were pieced from every conceivable scrap of fabric, ranging from bits of worn-out clothing, feed sacks, and pieces of bedding all the way to mohairs, woolens, cottons, silks, and brocades.

It's easy to understand why Log Cabins have remained dear to the hearts of quilters through the years. The blocks are quick and easy to cut and piece, and they make great use of bits of fabric tucked away in the scrap bag. A quilt made from blocks pieced on foundations doesn't require batting, which saves time, money, and quilting. And perhaps best of all, because there are so many wonderful variations possible, it's nearly impossible to run out of ways to make beautiful quilts.

The quilts in this book represent the best of a long-standing tradition of Log Cabins. Although the project directions have been updated to take advantage of the best technology has to offer, like the sewing machine and rotary cutter, keep in mind, as you build your blocks log by log, that you are also building on a wonderful part of our quiltmaking heritage.

Suzanne Nelson

Suzanne Nelson

LOG CABIN
PROJECTS

SUNSHINE AND SHADOW

Skill Level: *Easy*

The classic setting of this quilt emphasizes the half-light, half-dark division of the Log Cabin blocks. In this version, 3½-inch blocks make a sweet and simple crib quilt. As with many Log Cabin settings, the size of the quilt can be varied by simply changing the block size or the number of blocks.

BEFORE YOU BEGIN

The directions for this quilt are written based on using the foundation technique, which makes it easier to work with the small pieces in the wallhanging and crib quilt. The larger pieces in the twin-size quilt make it possible to use either the foundation method or the chain-piecing technique. Read the general construction directions in "Log Cabin Basics," beginning on page 118, to become familiar with the foundation technique. Prepare a foundation for each block using one of the patterns on pages 9–10. The 7-inch block pattern has been reduced; enlarge it 150 percent before tracing. If you prefer to use the chain-piecing technique, see page 121 for details.

CHOOSING FABRICS

In the quilt shown, red center squares and a red border are a perfect complement to the predominantly blue scrap fabrics, creating a warm, homespun feeling. But the fabric colors used in this scrappy quilt are not as important as their value, the term indicating how light or dark a color is. Select a group of light fabrics with the same basic value

Quilt Sizes

	Wallhanging	Crib (shown)	Twin
Finished Quilt Size	30½" × 30½"	37½" × 44½"	65½" × 79½"
Finished Block Size	3½"	3½"	7"
Number of Blocks	36	80	80

Materials

	Wallhanging	Crib	Twin
Dark prints	¾ yard	1⅛ yards	3¼ yards
Light prints	¾ yard	1¼ yards	2½ yards
Dark brown print	⅝ yard	¾ yard	1 yard
Red	⅜ yard	½ yard	¾ yard
Backing	1¼ yards	1½ yards	5 yards
Batting (optional)	36" × 36"	43" × 50"	71" × 85"
Binding	⅜ yard	½ yard	¾ yard
Foundation material	½ yard	⅞ yard	3¼ yards

NOTE: Yardages are based on 44/45-inch-wide fabrics that are at least 42 inches wide after preshrinking.

and a group of dark fabrics with the same basic value. Refer to page 120 in "Log Cabin Basics" for tips on grouping fabrics into categories based on color value.

To help develop your own unique color scheme for the quilt, make several photocopies of the **Color Plan** on page 11, and use crayons, colored pencils, or markers to experiment with different color arrangements.

Light and dark yardages given are generous estimates of the total yardage actually used in the quilt. Since small amounts of many fabrics are a key ingredient for a successful scrap quilt, you will likely begin with more yardage than indicated but not use all of it.

3

Cutting Chart

Fabric	Piece	Wallhanging		Crib		Twin	
		Strip Width	Number of Strips	Strip Width	Number of Strips	Strip Width	Number of Strips
Dark prints	Logs	1¼"	15	1¼"	33	1¾"	60
Light prints	Logs	1¼"	12	1¼"	26	1¾"	46
Dark brown print	Outer border	4"	4	4"	5	4"	8
Red	1 (center)	1"	1	1"	2	1½"	3
	Inner border	1¾"	4	1¾"	5	1¾"	8

CUTTING

Referring to the Cutting Chart, cut the number of strips needed. Cut all strips across the fabric width (crosswise grain). **Note:** Cut and sew one sample block before cutting all the pieces for the quilt.

Measurements for the borders include ¼-inch seam allowances. The cut sizes listed for the logs are slightly wider than the finished log size plus ¼-inch seam allowances. With the foundation method, it's easier to work with slightly wider strips. You may wish to decrease the width in ⅛-inch increments as you become more familiar with the technique, but don't cut pieces less than 1 inch wide for the wallhanging and crib quilt and less than 1½ inches wide for the twin quilt.

The number of dark and light strips needed for logs is estimated based on using full-width yardage. If you are using scraps, the number of strips needed will vary.

MAKING THE FOUNDATIONS

Step 1. Make a template by tracing one of the block patterns on pages 9–10.

Step 2. Following the instructions on page 123 in "Log Cabin Basics," transfer the pattern to your chosen foundation material. Make sure the marked lines are visible from the back side when you hold the foundation up to the light. Use the **Block Diagram** as a color guide and a reference for piecing order. Cut out the foundations, leaving a bit of extra material on all sides.

Sew Easy

If you have chosen to use the chain-piecing method without a foundation, you'll need to cut the logs to length before sewing them. Refer to the chart below to cut the strips into logs.

Even if you are using the foundation method, this list is useful as a guideline to determine whether a particular scrap of fabric is large enough. With the foundation method, of course, it is not necessary to precut the fabric to these sizes.

Log Number	Log Size	
	Wallhanging and Crib	Twin
1, 2	1" × 1"	1½" × 1½"
3, 4	1" × 1½"	1½" × 2½"
5, 6	1" × 2"	1½" × 3½"
7, 8	1" × 2½"	1½" × 4½"
9, 10	1" × 3"	1½" × 5½"
11, 12	1" × 3½"	1½" × 6½"
13	1" × 4"	1½" × 7½"

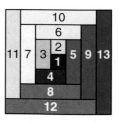

Block Diagram

PIECING THE BLOCKS

Make a sample block before cutting fabric for the entire quilt. If you experience problems while assembling the block, increase the strip width. Using strips that are slightly wider than necessary can be a real time-saver since not as much precision is needed when positioning them for sewing. Reevaluate your work often. You may find that strip width can be decreased again once you are more familiar with the method.

Step 1. Cut the centers of the blocks from the red strips. For the wallhanging and crib quilt, cut the 1-inch strips into 1-inch squares. For the twin-size quilt, cut the 1½-inch strips into 1½-inch squares.

Step 2. Place a red center square right side up on the back side of a foundation, covering the area of piece 1, as shown in **Diagram 1**. Secure with tape, a bit of glue stick, or a pin.

Hold the foundation up to the light with the back side away from you. You should be able to see a shadow of the center square through the foundation. Check to make sure it extends past all lines surrounding piece 1. If it doesn't, reposition the square and check again.

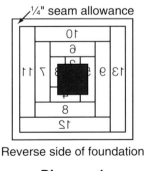

Reverse side of foundation

Diagram 1

Step 3. Select a light fabric for log 2. Place the strip right side down on top of the center square, aligning the top and left edges, as shown in **Diagram 2A**. (The strip will completely cover the red square.) Holding the fabric in position, flip the foundation to its front side and sew on the line separating pieces 1 and 2, as shown in **2B**. Begin and end the line of stitches approximately ⅛ inch on either side of the line.

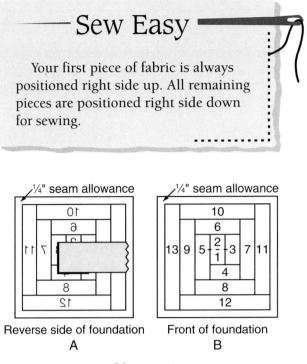
Reverse side of foundation   Front of foundation
A   B

Diagram 2

Step 4. Remove the foundation from the machine and flip it over to the back side. If you used tape to secure the center square, remove it now. Cut away the excess tail of fabric (cut just past the end of stitches, as shown in **Diagram 3A**). Trim the seam allowance if necessary to reduce bulk. Flip piece 2 into a right-side-up position, finger pressing it into place. See **3B**. Hold the foundation up to the light with the back side away from you. Check to make sure the shadow of piece 2 overlaps all unsewn lines around its perimeter.

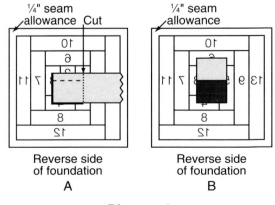

Reverse side of foundation   Reverse side of foundation
A   B

Diagram 3

Step 5. Select a light fabric for log 3, and position it right side down on log 2, as shown in

A small piece of wood (such as a Popsicle stick) makes a handy "iron." Press it along the seam as you flip pieces open.

Diagram 4A. Holding the strip in place, flip the foundation over and sew on the line separating pieces 1 and 2 from 3, again beginning and ending approximately 1/8 inch on either side of the line. Remove from the machine, trim the tail, and flip piece 3 into a right-side-up position, finger pressing it into place, as shown in **4B.** If necessary, trim excess bulk from the seam allowances.

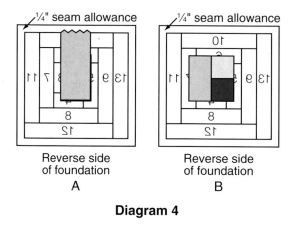

Reverse side of foundation
A

Reverse side of foundation
B

Diagram 4

The front of your foundation should now look like **Diagram 5.** Notice that the seam lines intersect each other. This crisscrossing of lines will continue, helping to stabilize your seams.

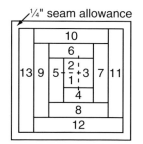

Diagram 5

Step 6. Continue to add pieces in numerical order, trimming seams to reduce bulk and finger pressing each piece open as you work. When adding pieces 10 through 13, make sure their edges will extend past the perimeter of the marked seam allowance when flipped right side up after sewing. After the last piece is sewn, press the block with a warm iron. Cut on the outermost line of the foundation.

Step 7. Repeat Steps 2 through 6, making the required number of blocks for your chosen quilt size.

ASSEMBLING THE QUILT TOP

Step 1. Use a design wall or flat surface to arrange your blocks into a pleasing design. Use the photo on page 2, one of the quilt diagrams (shown on the opposite page and page 8), or your own color drawing as a guide to block placement.

Step 2. When you are satisfied with the layout, sew the blocks into four-block units. First sew the blocks together in pairs, as shown in **Diagram 6,** pressing the seams in opposite directions. If you are using removable foundations, tear away the portion surrounding the seam allowances where blocks are joined.

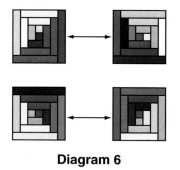

Diagram 6

Note: Permanent foundations create additional bulk in the seam allowance. If seams are too bulky to press to one side, it may be necessary to press them open. Be sure to match and pin pressed-open seams carefully when rows are joined.

Step 3. Referring to **Diagram 7,** sew the pairs together into a four-block unit.

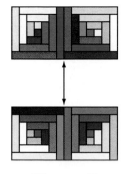

Diagram 7

Step 5. Sew the units into rows, as shown in **Diagram 8.** Make a total of three rows for the wallhanging or five rows for the crib and twin quilts.

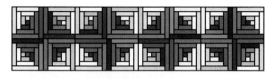

Diagram 8

Step 4. Repeat with the remaining blocks, making a total of 9 four-block units for the wallhanging or 20 four-block units for the crib and twin quilts. Be sure to place each sewn unit back into its proper position in your quilt layout.

Step 6. Referring to the quilt diagrams on this page and page 8, sew the rows together, carefully matching seams. Tear away any remaining removable foundation material from the seam allowances.

Crib- and Twin-Size Quilt Diagram

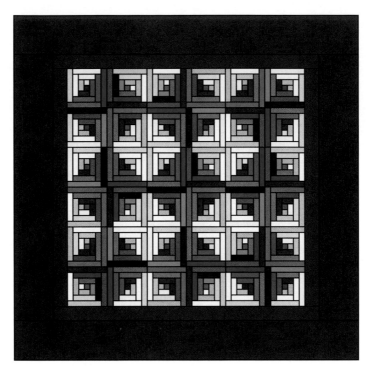

Wallhanging Diagram

ADDING THE BORDERS

The procedure for adding the borders is the same regardless of the quilt size you are making. For both the crib and twin quilts, however, you must first make long border strips.

Step 1. For the crib quilt, cut one of the red border strips in half, and sew one half each to two red border strips. You will have two long borders and two short borders. Repeat with the brown outer border strips. For the twin quilt, simply sew the border strips together in pairs. You will have four long red inner borders and four long dark brown outer borders.

Step 2. Measure the length of the quilt top, taking the measurement through the vertical center of the quilt rather than along the sides. Cut two 1¾-inch red border strips to the measured length.

Step 3. Fold one strip in half crosswise. Unfold it and position it right side down along one side of the quilt top, with the crease at the horizontal midpoint. Pin at the midpoint and ends first, then along the length of the entire side, easing in full-

ness if necessary. Sew the border to the quilt top using a ¼-inch seam allowance. Press the seam allowance toward the border. Repeat on the opposite side.

Step 4. Measure the width of the quilt, taking the measurement through the horizontal center of the quilt rather than along the edge. Cut the remaining two red border strips to this length.

Step 5. In the same manner as for the side borders, position and pin a strip along one end of the quilt top, easing in fullness if necessary. Stitch, using a ¼-inch seam allowance, and press the seam toward the border. Repeat on the opposite end of the quilt top.

Step 6. In the same manner as for the inner borders, add the dark brown outer border strips to the four sides of the quilt top.

QUILTING AND FINISHING

Step 1. Mark the quilt top for quilting. A fan design, sometimes called Baptist Fan, was used in the borders of this quilt. An X was quilted in the red center of each block. The logs were quilted lengthwise down the center, with lines intersecting and turning at the edges to create a series of squares.

Step 2. If you are making the twin-size quilt, you will have to piece the backing. Divide the 5-yard piece of fabric in half crosswise and trim the selvages. Cut one of the pieces in half lengthwise, and sew one half to each side of the full-width piece. Press the seams open.

Step 3. Layer the top, batting (if used), and backing. Baste the layers together.

Step 4. Quilt as desired.

Step 5. Referring to the directions on page 137 in "Quiltmaking Basics," make and attach double-fold binding. To calculate the amount of binding needed for the quilt size you are making, add up the length of the four sides of the quilt and add 9 inches. The total is the approximate number of inches of binding you will need.

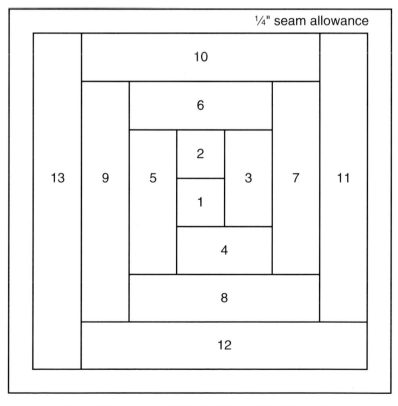

Block Pattern for Crib Quilt and Wallhanging

Pattern shown is the mirror image of the finished block.

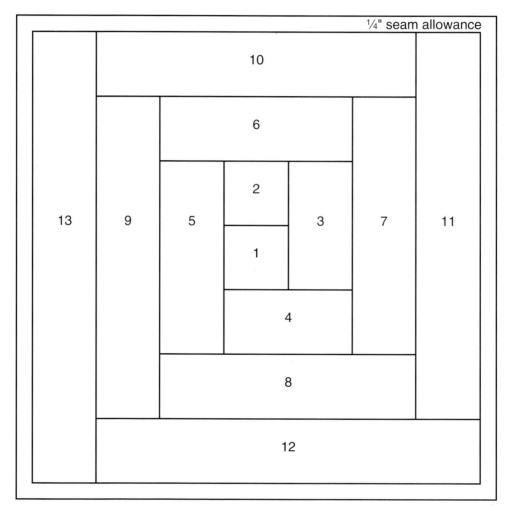

Block Pattern for Twin Quilt

Pattern shown is the mirror image of the finished block.
Note: Pattern is reduced. Enlarge it 150 percent before tracing.

SUNSHINE AND SHADOW
Color Plan

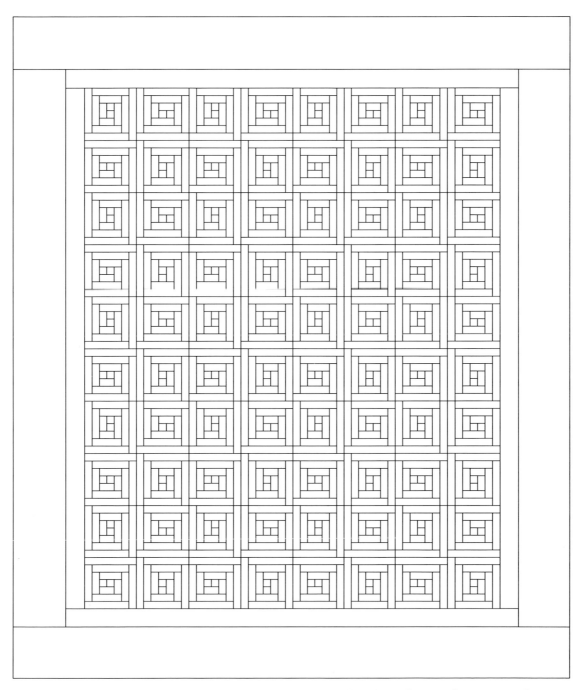

Photocopy this page and use it to experiment with color schemes for your quilt.

SCRAP HALF LOG CABIN
Skill Level: *Easy*

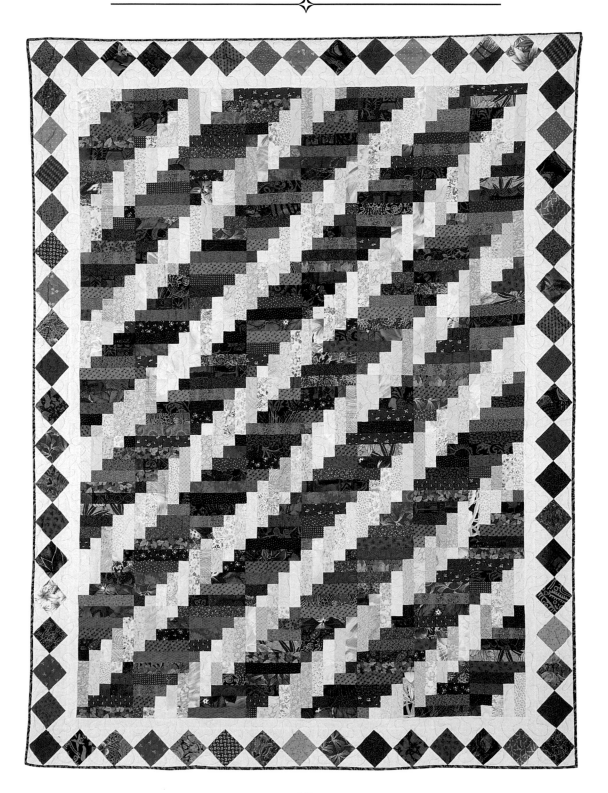

Deep, rich jewel tones fairly sparkle in this fast and fun twin-size scrap quilt. A pieced border adds new interest to the traditional Straight Furrows setting. The blocks, called Half Log Cabin or Off-Center Log Cabin, are built out from a corner square rather than a center square. Like traditional Log Cabin blocks, they're extremely versatile and can be arranged in a variety of settings.

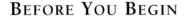

Before You Begin

The directions for this quilt are written based on using a unique piecing method developed by quiltmaker Sharyn Craig. It is a form of chain piecing, but instead of sewing all matching units at one time, you sew together varying stages of up to four blocks at a time. Once the first block is completed, you can produce blocks at a rate of about four to eight an hour, and each one will be different. The technique makes sewing this scrappy Log Cabin quilt fun and easy. Since the method may be a bit different from others you have used, we suggest you read through the instructions a few times before beginning.

Quilt Sizes

	Crib	Twin (shown)	Queen
Finished Quilt Size	43" × 58"	73" × 95½"	88" × 103"
Finished Block Size	7½"	7½"	7½"
Number of Blocks	24	88	120

Materials

	Crib	Twin	Queen
Dark fabrics	1½ yards	4¼ yards	5¼ yards
Light fabrics	¾ yard	2⅜ yards	3 yards
Light border fabric	1¼ yards	1⅝ yards	1⅞ yards
Backing	3 yards	5¾ yards	8¼ yards
Batting	47" × 62"	77" × 100"	92" × 107"
Binding	½ yard	⅝ yard	¾ yard

NOTE: Yardages are based on 44/45-inch-wide fabrics that are at least 42 inches wide after preshrinking.

Choosing Fabrics

The yardage requirements for light and dark logs is an approximation of the amounts actually used in the blocks. For a successful scrap quilt, variety is important, so you will likely start out with more yardage than indicated, but not all of it will be used.

Long strips of fabric are required for this method of block assembly. If you purchase new fabrics, select regular yardage cuts, not fat quarters. For best results, choose fabrics with lots of contrast. Including a few medium-value fabrics will add interest, but most of the fabrics should be either dark or light.

You can vary the look of the quilt by controlling the use of one or more of the fabrics. For example, you might use a single fabric for all of the light logs. Or you might reverse the positions of the light and dark fabrics—start with a light square instead of a dark one, and the resulting quilt will have a lighter overall effect.

To help develop your own unique color scheme for the quilt, photocopy the **Color Plan** on page 21, and use crayons or colored pencils to experiment with different color arrangements.

CUTTING

All measurements include ¼-inch seam allowances. Referring to the Cutting Chart, cut the strips and squares needed for which quilt size you are making. Cut one or two strips from each fabric to begin with. The total number of strips you use from each piece will depend on the number of different fabrics you've chosen to work with. Cut all strips across the fabric width (crosswise grain). Accurate cutting is critical to this piecing technique, so measure and cut all strips carefully.

Cutting Chart				
Crib				
Fabric	2" Strips	4" Squares	3⅜" Squares	6¼" Squares
Dark fabrics	16	38		
Light fabrics	11			
Light border fabric	5		8	17
Twin				
Fabric	2" Strips	4" Squares	3⅜" Squares	6¼" Squares
Dark fabrics	57	64		
Light fabrics	39			
Light border fabric	8		8	30
Queen				
Fabric	2" Strips	4" Squares	3⅜" Squares	6¼" Squares
Dark fabrics	75	74		
Light fabrics	51			
Light border fabric	9		8	35

PIECING THE BLOCKS

Step 1. Sort the fabric strips into a light pile and a dark pile, and trim the selvage from one end of each strip, squaring up that end. Don't worry about color placement as you assemble blocks; just think of the fabrics in terms of light and dark. A fabric that doesn't look quite right in a single block won't even be noticeable when the quilt is assembled. There are four basic steps to assembling the blocks:

1. **Sew** the units to a strip;
2. **Cut** the units apart;
3. **Press** the seam allowance;
4. **Stack** the sewn units on top of each other.

These four steps are the key to this piecing system. Follow them carefully when assembling the blocks. The numbers on the **Block Diagram** show the order in which strips are added. In the quilt shown, the odd numbers are dark strips and the even numbers are light strips.

Step 2. Pick up a dark strip. Use your rotary cutter to cut a 2-inch square from the trimmed end, then set the remainder of the strip aside. (Begin all steps with the trimmed, squared-up end of the strips.)

Block Diagram

Step 3. Pick up a light strip. Position it right side up in front of you. Position the dark 2-inch square right side down on top of your light strip. Sew them together, as shown in **Diagram 1A,** using a ¼-inch seam allowance.

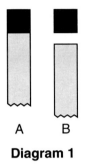

A   B
Diagram 1

Step 4. Cut the light strip at the bottom edge of the dark 2-inch square, as shown in **1B.** The resulting sewn piece, containing a dark and a light portion, is called a unit.

Step 5. Press the seam allowance toward the newest fabric, in this case the light.

Step 6. Position the pressed unit, right side down, on your sewing table, as shown in **Diagram 2.** Pay close attention to the placement of the light and dark portions.

Step 7. Pick up a dark strip of fabric. Make sure it's different from the one you used to start the block. Position it right side up at the machine.

— Sew Easy —

Here's a pressing technique that will help prevent stretching and distorting the unit. Place the unopened unit on the ironing board with the newest fabric on top and the sewn edge away from you. Press with the iron to "set" the stitches. Lift the top piece to open up the unit. Set the iron on the portion nearest you, then glide it gently toward the new fabric to direct the seam allowance toward the newest fabric.

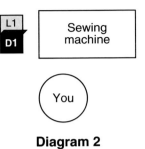

Diagram 2

Pick up the sewn unit and place it right side down directly on top of your new dark strip. Be careful not to change the position of your sewn unit; the newest (light) strip should still be positioned at the top, as shown in **Diagram 3.** Align the top edge of the sewn unit with the trimmed end of the dark strip.

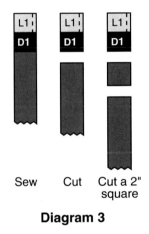

Sew   Cut   Cut a 2"
                    square
Diagram 3

Step 8. Sew the pieces together along the right-hand edge, using a ¼-inch seam allowance. Cut the dark strip at the bottom edge of the unit, as shown in the diagram. Press the seam allowance toward the newest strip.

Step 9. Cut a 2-inch square from the end of the dark strip. This new square is the start of your second block. From this point on, every time you add a new dark fabric to your blocks, you will cut a 2-inch starter square from it.

Step 10. Position the pieced unit and the new dark square right side down, as illustrated in **Diagram 4** on page 16, with the newest dark fabric (D2) in the bottom position. Stack the new starter square on top of the unit as shown, placing it on the strip of fabric it matches. You will not sew the extra square to the unit—stacking the units in this way will help you remember fabric position, which will become increasingly important as blocks are assembled.

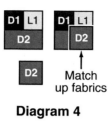

Diagram 4

Step 11. Place a new light strip right side up at the sewing machine. Pick up the stack and position the two units on the new light strip, as shown in **Diagram 5**. Make sure both units are aligned with the right-hand edge of the new light strip.

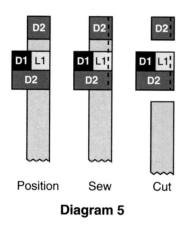

Position   Sew   Cut

Diagram 5

Step 12. Sew the pieces together using a ¼-inch seam allowance. Cut the light strip at the bottom edge of the unit, then cut the units apart, as shown in **Diagram 5**. Press the seam allowance toward the newest strip. You now have partial units for two blocks. **Diagram 6** shows the partial units (right side down).

Stacking the units correctly is the most important step for accurate block assembly. Always fol-

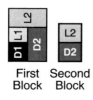

First   Second
Block   Block

Diagram 6

low this rule: If the last fabric added was a *light* fabric, stack the units with that new light fabric in the *top* position (away from you). If the last fabric added was a *dark* fabric, stack the units with that new dark fabric in the *bottom* position (toward you).

Step 13. Stack the two units, as shown in **Diagram 7**, making sure the newest light fabric (L2) pieces are matched up and in the top position.

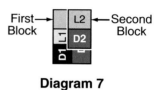

Diagram 7

Step 14. Place a new dark strip right side up at the sewing machine. Pick up the stack and position the two units right side down on the new dark strip, as shown in **Diagram 8**. Make sure both units are aligned with the right-hand edge of the new dark strip. Sew the pieces together using a ¼-inch seam allowance. Cut the dark strip at the bottom edge of the unit, then cut the units apart, as shown in the diagram. Press the seam allowance toward the newest strip.

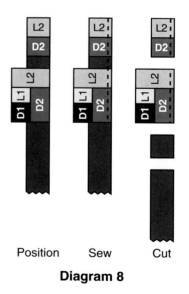

Position   Sew   Cut

Diagram 8

Step 15. Cut a new 2-inch square from the dark strip. You now have partial units for three blocks. See **Diagram 9** (shown right side down).

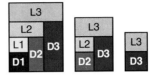

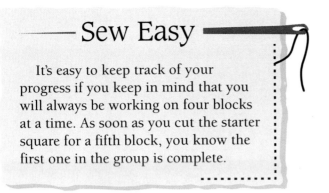

Sew Easy

It's easy to keep track of your progress if you keep in mind that you will always be working on four blocks at a time. As soon as you cut the starter square for a fifth block, you know the first one in the group is complete.

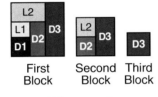

First   Second   Third
Block   Block   Block

Diagram 9

Step 16. Stack the units, matching fabrics. The last fabric added was dark (D3), so stack the units with that fabric in the bottom position, as shown in **Diagram 10.**

Diagram 10

Step 17. Place a new light strip right side up at the sewing machine. Position the stacked units right side down on the new strip, as shown in **Diagram 11.** Make sure the units are aligned with the right-hand edge of the new light strip.

Diagram 11

Step 18. Sew, cut the units apart, and press as described. The three units should now look like those in **Diagram 12** (shown right side down).

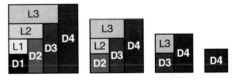

Diagram 12

Step 19. Stack the units, matching like fabrics as before. The last fabric added was light (L3); place it in the top position. Put a new dark strip in place at the sewing machine and position the units right side down on top of it, keeping them in correct position.

Step 20. Sew, cut, and press. Cut an extra 2-inch square. You now have units for four Half Log Cabin blocks. See **Diagram 13** (shown right side down).

Diagram 13

Step 21. In the same manner, add another light strip, then another dark strip. With the addition of this dark strip, you will complete the first block and begin the fifth block.

Look at the completed block, the three unfinished units, and the newest 2-inch square, shown right side down in **Diagram 14.** Even though some of the fabrics repeat, their position in each block varies. As you continue making blocks and then arranging them with others into a setting, the repetition won't be obvious. The end result will be a true scrap quilt, with randomly placed fabrics.

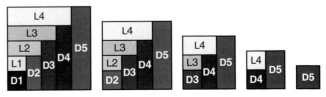

Diagram 14

Step 22. Continue adding strips in this manner until you have completed the required number of blocks for your chosen quilt size.

ASSEMBLING THE QUILT TOP

Step 1. Use a design wall or flat surface to arrange your blocks into a pleasing design. Use the photo on page 12, the **Twin-Size Quilt Diagram**, or your own shaded drawing as a guide to block placement. The quilt diagram illustrates the layout of the twin-size quilt, which consists of 11 rows with 8 blocks in each row. Except for the number of blocks, the layout for the other two sizes is the same. The crib quilt is arranged in 6 rows with 4 blocks in each row, and the queen-size quilt consists of 12 rows with 10 blocks in each row.

Step 2. When you are satisfied with the layout, sew the blocks into rows, as shown by the dark horizontal lines in the **Twin-Size Quilt Diagram**, pressing the seam allowances in opposite directions from row to row.

Step 3. Sew the rows together, carefully matching seams where blocks meet. If you've pressed the seam allowances in opposite directions, the seams should fit tightly against each other, helping you achieve a perfect match. Press the seams where rows were joined.

MAKING THE PIECED BORDER

Step 1. Cut the 3⅜-inch light fabric squares in half diagonally, as shown in **Diagram 15A**, producing two triangles per square. Cut the 6¼-inch light fabric squares diagonally both ways, as shown in **15B**, producing four triangles per square. Keep the resulting triangles in separate stacks to avoid confusion.

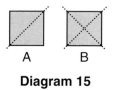

Diagram 15

Step 2. Sew a small triangle (from a 3⅜-inch square) to two sides of a 4-inch dark square, as shown in **Diagram 16A**. Press the seams toward the dark square. Add a large triangle (from a 6¼-inch square) to the unit, as shown in **16B**. Press. Make a total of eight of these units and set them aside for now; they will form the ends of the borders.

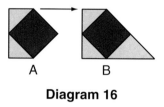

A   B

Diagram 16

Step 3. Sew a large triangle from a 6¼-inch square to two sides of the remaining 4-inch dark squares, as shown in **Diagram 17**. Press the seams toward the dark squares.

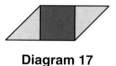

Diagram 17

Step 4. To assemble the side borders, sew the Step 3 units together, as shown in **Diagram 18**. Continue adding units until the strip reaches the required length. For the crib quilt, join 8 units; for the twin-size quilt, sew together 15 units; for the queen-size quilt, join 17 units. Repeat, making a second strip containing the same number of units.

Diagram 18

Step 5. Referring to **Diagram 19**, sew a Step 2 unit to each end of each side border strip. The side borders are now complete.

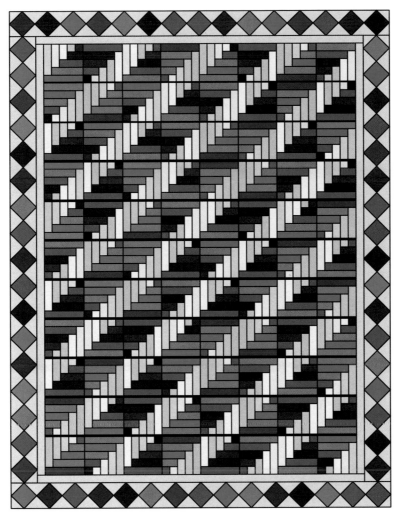

Twin-Size Quilt Diagram

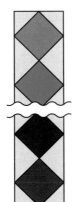

Diagram 19

Step 6. To make the top and bottom borders, sew Step 3 units together as described previously. For the crib quilt, join 7 units for each strip; for the twin-size quilt, join 13 units for each; for the queen-size quilt, sew together 16 units for each strip.

Step 7. Sew a Step 2 unit to each end of each border strip to complete the top and bottom borders.

ADDING THE BORDERS

The procedure for adding the borders to the quilt is the same regardless of which quilt size you've chosen to make. However, the narrow inner border is prepared differently for each of the three sizes.

Step 1. For the crib quilt, cut one 2-inch-wide border strip in half crosswise, and sew one half each to two of the remaining strips. You will have two long borders and two shorter borders. For the twin-size quilt, sew the 2-inch-wide border strips together in pairs, making four long borders of equal length. And for the queen-size quilt, sew the border strips together in pairs, then divide the remaining strip in half crosswise and sew one half each to two of the long strips.

Step 2. Measure the quilt from top to bottom, taking the measurement through the vertical center of the quilt, not at the sides. Cut the two longest border strips to this length.

Step 3. Fold one strip in half crosswise and crease. Unfold it and position it right side down along one side of the quilt top, with the crease at the horizontal midpoint. Pin at the midpoint and ends first, then along the length of the entire side, easing in fullness if necessary. Sew the border to the quilt using a ¼-inch seam allowance. Press the seam allowance toward the border. Repeat on the opposite side.

Step 4. Measure the width of the quilt, taking the measurement through the horizontal center of the quilt and including the side borders. Cut the remaining two border strips to this length.

Step 5. In the same manner as for the side borders, position and pin a strip along one end of the quilt top, easing in fullness if necessary. Stitch, using a ¼-inch seam allowance. Press the seam toward the border. Repeat on the opposite end.

Step 6. Determine the midpoint of the side pieced borders, pin in position, and stitch them to the quilt.

Step 7. Determine the midpoint of the top and bottom pieced borders, and add them to the quilt in the same manner. The completed quilt top should look like the one shown in the **Twin-Size Quilt Diagram.**

QUILTING AND FINISHING

Step 1. Mark the quilt top for quilting. The quilt shown in the photo was machine quilted in an allover meandering pattern.

Step 2. Regardless of which quilt size you've chosen to make, the backing will have to be pieced. To make the most efficient use of yardage, piece the back for the crib and queen-size quilts

with the seams running horizontally across the quilt. For the twin-size quilt, piece the back with the seams running vertically. **Diagram 20** illustrates the three quilt backs. Begin by trimming the selvages and dividing the yardage into equal pieces. For the crib and twin sizes, you need two equal pieces. For the queen size, divide the yardage into three equal pieces.

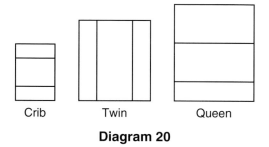

Crib   Twin   Queen

Diagram 20

Step 3. For the crib quilt, divide one of the backing pieces in half lengthwise, and sew one narrow piece to each side of the full-width piece. Press the seams open. Layer the backing, batting, and quilt top, making sure the seams of the backing run horizontally across the quilt.

Step 4. For the twin-size quilt, divide one of the pieces in half lengthwise, and sew one narrow piece to each side of the full-width piece. Press the seams open. Layer the backing, batting, and quilt top.

Step 5. The queen-size backing should be at least 96 × 111 inches. Sew two full-width pieces together and measure their width. Subtract that figure from 111 inches to determine the width you need to cut from the third strip. Cut the strip and sew it to the joined section. Press the seams open. Layer the backing, batting, and quilt top, making sure the seams of the backing run horizontally across the quilt.

Step 6. Baste the layers together. Quilt as desired.

Step 7. Referring to the directions on page 137 in "Quiltmaking Basics," make and attach double-fold binding. To calculate the amount of binding needed for which quilt size you are making, add up the length of the four sides of the quilt and add 9 inches. The total is the approximate number of inches of binding you will need.

SCRAP HALF LOG CABIN
Color Plan

Photocopy this page and use it to experiment with color schemes for your quilt.

PINEAPPLE LOG CABIN
Skill Level: *Intermediate*

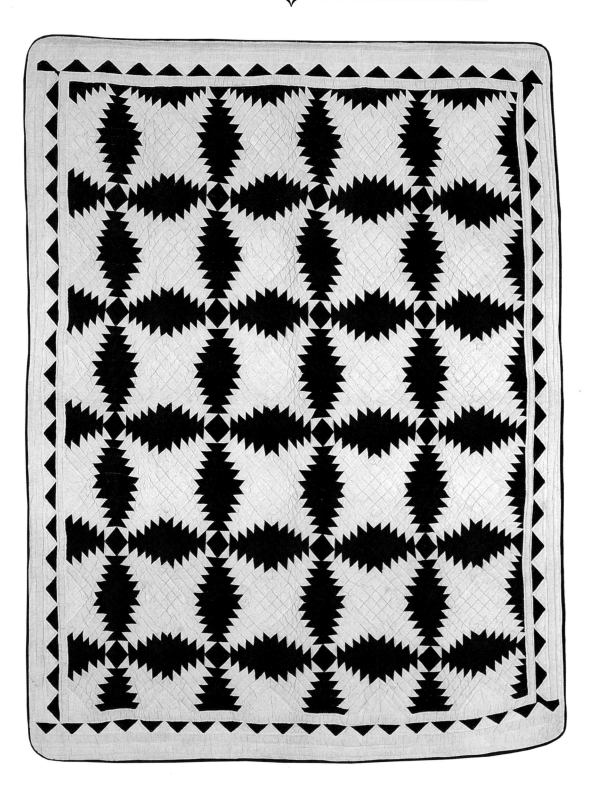

Two-color quilts have long been popular with quiltmakers, and strong graphic images like the one created by the Pineapple block gained a large following at the end of the nineteenth century. Although the exact provenance of this striking double quilt is unknown, it is thought to have been made in southeastern Missouri around 1920. While the incomplete block layout and the quirky borders add a charming touch to this quilt, the instructions are written so that the design is complete on all sides and the pieced borders meet at the corners.

BEFORE YOU BEGIN

The directions for this quilt are written based on using the foundation method, which makes it easier to achieve the precise piecing needed. Read through the general construction directions in "Log Cabin Basics," beginning on page 118, to become familiar with the foundation technique. Prepare a foundation for each block using the full-size pattern on page 32.

We recommend using paper or another rigid, removable foundation for this quilt. Muslin foundations sometimes "shrink" slightly as you work, due to the slight tucking that takes place when each seam is sewn. For many quilts, this variation causes no problems. For this quilt, even a slight difference in block size—multiplied by the number of blocks involved—can create problems when you add the pieced inner borders. Because paper foundations remain rigid, each finished block will be very close to the exact size of the original template.

Quilt Sizes

	Crib	Double (shown)	King
Finished Quilt Size	50¾" × 62¾"	74¾" × 86¾"	98¾" × 98¾"
Finished Whole Block Size	12"	12"	12"
Number of Blocks			
Whole blocks	6	20	36
Half blocks	10	18	24
Quarter blocks	4	4	4

Materials

	Crib	Double	King
Red	2½ yards	5⅜ yards	8¼ yards
White	3 yards	5⅞ yards	8½ yards
Backing	3½ yards	5½ yards	9 yards
Batting (optional)	57" × 69"	81" × 93"	105" × 105"
Binding	½ yard	⅝ yard	¾ yard

NOTE: Yardages are based on 44/45-inch-wide fabrics that are at least 42 inches wide after preshrinking.

CHOOSING FABRICS

The simple two-color scheme of this quilt can be created with any two high-contrast fabrics. Or make it as a scrap quilt: Use white in the same areas as in this quilt and replace the red with dark scraps.

To help develop your own unique color scheme for the quilt, photocopy the **Color Plan** on page 31, and use crayons or colored pencils to experiment with different color arrangements.

Cutting Chart

Fabric	Piece	Strip Width	Number of Strips		
			Crib	Double	King
White	Logs	1¾"	24	60	98
	Block corners	4⅞"	3	8	13
	Inner border	2"	5	7	8
	Outer border	4¼"	6	8	10
	Pieced border	5⅝"	2	3	4
		4⅛"	1	1	1
Red	Centers	2½"	2	3	4
	Logs	1¾"	36	90	147
	Pieced border	5⅝"	3	3	5

CUTTING

Referring to the Cutting Chart, cut the number of strips needed. Cut all strips across the fabric width (crosswise grain). The measurements for the borders include ¼-inch seam allowances.

The cut sizes for the logs are slightly wider than the finished log size plus ¼-inch seam allowances. With the foundation method, it's easier to work with slightly wider strips. You may wish to decrease the width in ⅛-inch increments as you become more familiar with the technique, but don't cut pieces less than 1 inch wide.

To make the block centers, cut the 2½-inch-wide red strips into 2½-inch squares. To make the block corner triangles, cut the 4⅞-inch-wide white strips into 4⅞-inch squares, then cut the squares in half diagonally. **Note:** Cut and sew one sample block before cutting all of the pieces for the quilt.

MAKING THE FOUNDATIONS

Step 1. One-quarter of the pattern for the Pineapple block is given full size on page 32. This quilt contains quarter blocks, half blocks, and whole blocks; make a template for each type of block, as shown in the **Block Diagram.** Trace the pattern as it is for the quarter-block template; trace it twice and join the pieces for the half-block template; trace it four times and carefully join the

pieces to make the whole-block template. To make it easier to match the sections, the pattern is given without seam allowances; add a ¼-inch seam allowance to all sides of each completed template.

At the same time, make a template from pattern A on page 33. Set this template aside for now; you will use it later when making the pieced borders.

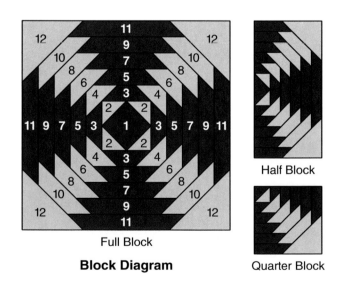

Full Block

Block Diagram

Half Block

Quarter Block

Step 2. Following the instructions on page 123 in "Log Cabin Basics," transfer the pattern to your chosen foundation material. Use the **Block Diagram** as a reference for piecing order, transferring the numbers from the full-block diagram to the foundations. Cut out the foundations, leaving a bit of extra material on all sides.

— Sew Easy

Here's an easy way to keep track of where you are in the piecing: In this block, all even-numbered rounds contain white fabric and all odd-numbered rounds contain red fabric.

PIECING THE BLOCKS

Make a sample block before cutting fabric for the entire quilt. If you experience problems while assembling the block, increase the strip width slightly. Using strips slightly wider than necessary can be a real time-saver since not as much precision is required when positioning them for sewing. Reevaluate your work often. You may find that strip width can be decreased again once you are more familiar with the method.

Choose a full-block foundation from your stack. You will position fabric on its reverse side and sew on the front of the foundation, directly on the marked lines. Make sure you can see the marked lines from the back side when you hold the foundation up to the light.

Begin piecing the Pineapple block at its center, working outward in a clockwise or counterclockwise direction as you add red and white strips. The center piece is always positioned first, right side up. Add other pieces in the order indicated on the template. An entire round or row of white pieces will be sewn, then an entire round of red pieces.

Sometimes it's helpful to make a mock-up foundation to use as a piecing reference. Premarking areas as red or white, or shading them with a pencil if you're using paper, will make piecing speedier and help ensure correct placement.

Step 1. Position a red center square on the back side of your foundation, centered right side up, over the area for piece 1, as shown in **Diagram 1.** Secure the fabric with tape, a bit of glue stick, or a pin.

Hold the foundation up to the light with the back side away from you. You should be able to

see a shadow of the red square through the foundation. Check to make sure it extends past all lines surrounding piece 1.

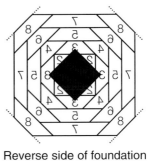

Reverse side of foundation
Center of block shown only

Diagram 1

Step 2. Row 2 is assembled with white fabric. Place the end of a white strip right side down on top of the center piece, aligning the edge of the white fabric with the edge of the red square, as shown in **Diagram 2A.** If the beginning red square is in the proper position, an adequate seam allowance will be created when the seam is stitched.

Holding the white strip in position, flip the foundation over. Sew on the line separating piece 1 from the piece you are adding in Row 2, beginning and ending the stitches approximately ⅛ inch on either side of the line. See **2B.**

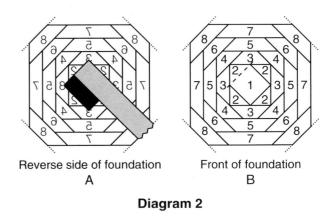

Reverse side of foundation   Front of foundation
A   B

Diagram 2

Step 3. Remove the foundation from the machine and turn it over to the back side. If you used tape to secure the center piece, remove it now. Cut away the excess tail of white fabric (cut just past the end of the line of stitches, as shown in **Diagram 3A**). Don't worry about angling the cut to match the correct shape of the piece; the piece will automatically be trimmed to shape when you add and trim Row 3. If necessary, even up and trim excess bulk from the seam allowance joining the two pieces you just sewed together.

Flip the white piece into a right-side-up position and finger press it into place, as shown in **3B**. Hold the foundation up to the light with the back side away from you. Check to make sure the shadow of the white piece overlaps all unsewn lines around its perimeter.

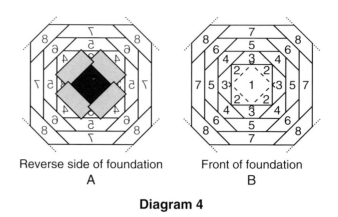

Reverse side of foundation
A

Front of foundation
B

Diagram 4

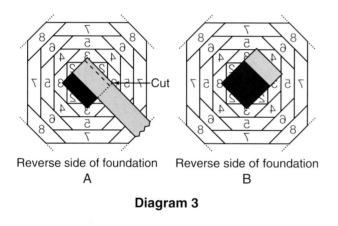

Reverse side of foundation
A

Reverse side of foundation
B

Diagram 3

Step 4. Add the next piece in Row 2 in exactly the same manner, aligning a white strip of fabric face down on the back side of the foundation, this time covering the next triangle in Row 2. (You can add pieces in either a clockwise or counterclockwise direction.)

Holding the fabric in place, turn the foundation face up and stitch on the diagonal line separating the new white piece from the red center. Flip the piece into a right-side-up position and finger press it into place. Check to make sure the fabric overlaps all sewing lines for that piece.

Step 5. Add the remaining two pieces in Row 2 in exactly the same manner. The front and back of your foundation should now look like **Diagram 4**.

Step 6. Now add Row 3, beginning with any piece and working in a circular direction. The front and back of your foundation should look

like **Diagram 5**, with the correct shape of pieces in Row 2 now recognizable. The squared, bulky edges remaining in Row 2 will be eliminated when you trim seam allowances for Row 3.

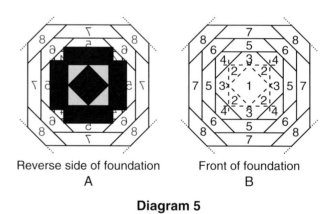

Reverse side of foundation
A

Front of foundation
B

Diagram 5

Step 7. Continue adding rows in exactly the same manner. Pieces in Rows 11 and 12 make up the outer border of your block. When sewing these rows to your foundation, make sure all the pieces extend a bit past the outer line of the seam allowance when flipped into place. When the block is finished, press lightly, then cut exactly on the outer lines of the marked seam allowance. Do not remove the foundation.

Step 8. Repeat Steps 1 through 7, making the required number of whole, half, and quarter blocks for your quilt. The piecing process for the half blocks and quarter blocks is the same as for the whole blocks.

ASSEMBLING THE QUILT TOP

Step 1. Use a design wall or flat surface to arrange your blocks, referring to the **Double-Size Quilt Diagram** or your own shaded drawing as a guide to block placement.

The quilt diagram illustrates the layout of the double quilt, which consists of seven rows. The top and bottom rows each contain two quarter blocks and four horizontal half blocks, and the five remaining rows each contain four whole blocks and two vertical half blocks.

Except for the number of blocks, the layout for the other two sizes is the same. The crib quilt consists of five rows. The top and bottom rows each contain two quarter blocks and two half blocks, and the three remaining rows each contain two whole blocks and two half blocks. The king-size quilt is made up of eight rows. The top and bottom rows each contain two quarter blocks and six half blocks. The six remaining rows each contain six whole blocks and two vertical half blocks.

Step 2. Sew the blocks into rows, as shown in **Diagram 6** on page 28. Remove the foundations from the seam allowances. Press the seam allowances in opposite directions from row to row.

Step 3. Join the rows, carefully matching the seams.

Double-Size Quilt Diagram

Row 1

Row 2

Row 3

Row 4

Row 5

Row 6

Row 7

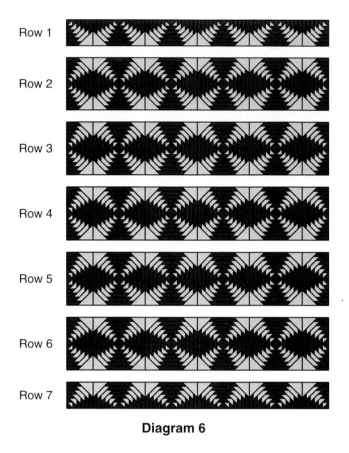

Diagram 6

MAKING THE PIECED BORDER

Step 1. The pieced border is made up of alternating red and white triangles. Cut the 5⅝-inch-wide strips into 5⅝-inch squares. Cut the squares diagonally both ways, as shown in **Diagram 7**. Handle the triangles carefully to avoid stretching. Place the A template over each triangle, aligning it with the corner, then trim off the excess fabric along the long straight edge of the triangle. Cutting the triangles from squares in this manner means the longest side of the triangle is on the straight of grain. This puts the most stable side of the triangle where you need it most—on the outer edge of the border.

Diagram 7

Step 2. Lay out the correct number of triangles for each border strip, beginning and ending each

strip with a red triangle. For the crib quilt, the top and bottom borders each contain 13 red and 12 white triangles. The side borders each contain 17 red and 16 white triangles. For the double quilt, the top and bottom borders each contain 15 red and 14 white triangles, while the side borders contain 18 red and 17 white triangles. For the king-size quilt, each of the four border strips contains 29 red and 28 white triangles.

Step 3. Using an exact ¼-inch seam allowance, sew the triangles together, as shown in **Diagram 8**. Piece the borders carefully; if they are not sewn accurately, they will not fit the completed quilt top. Press carefully to open the pieces to their full width; press the seams toward the red triangles. Set the pieced borders aside for now.

Diagram 8

ADDING THE BORDERS

In addition to the pieced border, the quilt has two plain borders—one on each side of the pieced border. To achieve the needed length, the border strips must be sewn together end to end. Prepare the plain borders as described here, then add all three borders to the quilt.

Step 1. To prepare the inner borders for the crib quilt, cut one of the 2-inch-wide inner border strips in half crosswise. Sew one half each to two of the remaining 2-inch-wide strips. For the outer borders, cut two of the 4¼-inch-wide outer border strips in half crosswise. Sew one half each to the four remaining strips.

To prepare the inner borders for the double quilt, cut one of the 2-inch-wide strips in half crosswise, and sew one half each to two other strips. Sew the remaining four strips together in pairs. For the outer border, sew the eight 4¼-inch-wide strips together in pairs.

To prepare the inner borders for the king-size quilt, sew the eight 2-inch-wide strips together in pairs. For the outer borders, sew eight of the 4¼-inch-wide strips together in pairs. Cut the two remaining strips in half crosswise, and sew one half each to the four long border strips.

Step 2. Measure the quilt from top to bottom, taking the measurement through the vertical center of the quilt, not at the sides. Cut two inner border strips to this length.

Step 3. Fold one strip in half crosswise and crease. Unfold it and position it right side down along one side of the quilt top, with the crease at the horizontal midpoint. Pin at the midpoint and ends first, then along the length of the entire side, easing in fullness if necessary. Sew the border to the quilt top using a ¼-inch seam allowance. Press the seam toward the border. Repeat on the opposite side.

Step 4. Measure the width of the quilt, taking the measurement through the horizontal center of the quilt and including the side borders. Cut the remaining two inner border strips to this length.

Step 5. In the same manner as for the side borders, position and pin a strip along one end of the quilt top, easing in fullness if necessary. Stitch, using a ¼-inch seam allowance. Press the seam toward the border. Repeat on the opposite end.

Step 6. To add the pieced borders, first check the length of the border strips against the quilt top. Even with careful sewing, the pieced borders may not fit exactly. If the borders are slightly longer than needed, ease in the extra fullness when pinning the strip in place. If the borders are slightly shorter than needed, it may be necessary to let out one or more of the seams very slightly. Be careful not to let out too much from any one seam.

Step 7. Sew on the side borders first, finding the midpoint, pinning, and sewing each strip in

place as you did with the inner borders. In the same manner, sew on the top and bottom pieced borders.

Step 8. To make the border corner triangles, cut four 4⅛-inch squares from the 4⅛-inch white strip. Cut each square in half diagonally. Referring to **Diagram 9**, fold each resulting triangle in half to find its midpoint. (The triangles are a bit larger than necessary and will be trimmed back after sewing.)

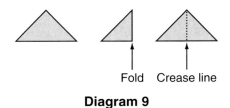

Fold   Crease line

Diagram 9

Step 9. Beginning at any corner, match the crease of a triangle to the intersection of the two red triangles at the ends of the border strips, as shown in **Diagram 10A**. Pin the triangle right side down along the edge and sew it to the quilt using a ¼-inch seam allowance. Press the seam toward the white triangle; the triangle is larger than necessary, so it will extend beyond the edge of the pieced border, as shown in **10B**.

Step 10. Use a plastic ruler to square up the corners, cutting each side flush with the edge of the pieced border. The finished corner should look like the one shown in **10C**.

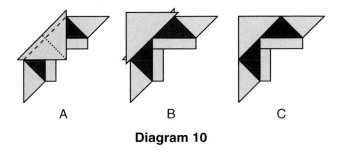

A   B   C

Diagram 10

Step 11. Measure, cut, and stitch the outer side borders in the same way that you added the inner borders and the pieced borders. Then add the top and bottom outer borders.

Step 12. Carefully remove any remaining foundation material. Don't tug too hard or you could distort seams.

Quilting and Finishing

Step 1. Mark the quilt top for quilting, if desired. The antique quilt shown has both in-the-ditch quilting and outline quilting, with a 1-inch grid quilted where the white corner triangles of the blocks come together.

········Sew **Q**uick·········

Use masking tape as a guideline for quilting grids and other straight lines. It saves time and effort by eliminating the need for marking. Each piece of tape can be reused several times.

Step 2. Regardless of which quilt size you've chosen to make, the backing will have to be pieced. **Diagram 11** illustrates the three quilt backs. For the crib quilt, you'll make the most efficient use of the yardage by piecing the back with the seams running horizontally across the quilt. For the double and king-size quilts, the seams run vertically.

Step 3. For the crib quilt, divide the 3½-yard piece of backing fabric in half crosswise and trim the selvages. Cut one of the pieces in half lengthwise, and sew one half to each side of the full-width piece. Press the seams open.

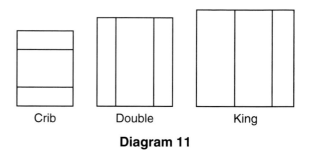

Crib   Double   King

Diagram 11

Step 4. For the double quilt, divide the 5½-yard piece of backing fabric in half crosswise and trim the selvages. Divide one of the pieces in half lengthwise, and sew one narrow piece to each side of the full-width piece. Press the seams open.

Step 5. For the king-size quilt, divide the 9-yard piece of backing fabric into three equal segments of approximately 108 inches each. Trim the selvages. The quilt back should measure approximately 108 inches square. Sew two of the segments together lengthwise and press the seam open. Measure the width of the pieced unit and subtract that number from 108 inches. Cut a strip this width from the remaining segment, and sew it to one side of the pieced backing. Press the seam open.

Step 6. Layer the backing, batting if used, and quilt top. Baste the layers together. Quilt as desired.

Step 7. Referring to the directions on page 137 in "Quiltmaking Basics," make and attach double-fold binding. To calculate the amount of binding needed for the quilt size you are making, add up the length of the four sides of the quilt and add 9 inches. The total is the approximate number of inches of binding you will need.

PINEAPPLE LOG CABIN

Color Plan

Photocopy this page and use it to experiment with color schemes for your quilt.

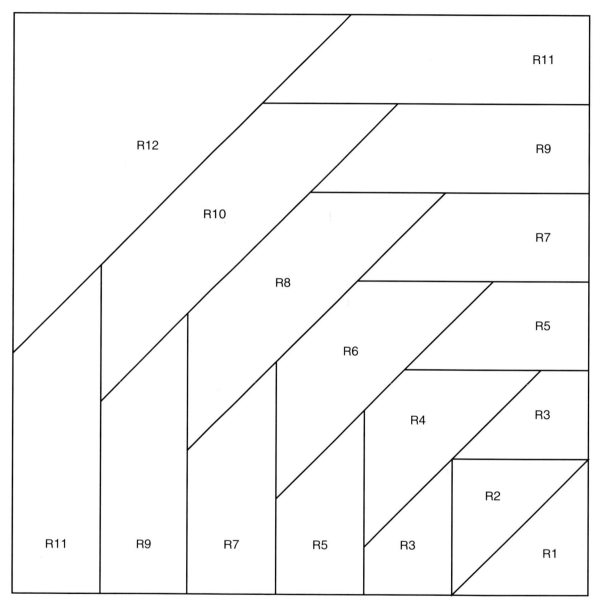

Quarter-Block Pattern

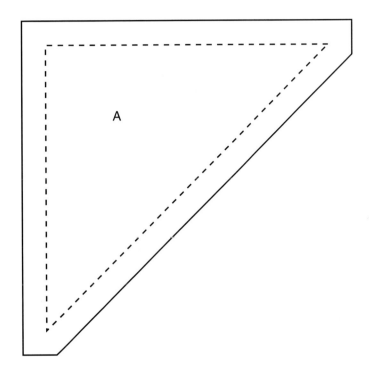

A

Nineteenth-Century Amish Log Cabin

Skill Level: *Challenging*

This sparkling quilt is an explosion of color and movement. While the deep, rich colors are traditional, the way they're used is not: Instead of making all the blocks half dark and half light, the quiltmaker mixed the colors and values in each block of this twin-size quilt. The creative use of Off-Center Log Cabin blocks creates the appearance of mitered corners on the pieced outer border.

BEFORE YOU BEGIN

The directions for this quilt are written based on using the foundation method, which will make piecing the small blocks much easier. Read through the general construction directions in "Log Cabin Basics," beginning on page 118, to become familiar with the foundation technique. Prepare a foundation for each block and corner block using the patterns on page 42. If you prefer to use the chain-piecing technique, see page 121 for details.

CHOOSING FABRICS

This quilt is comprised of only solid-color fabrics in what are generally thought of as Amish colors: blues, purples, greens, and reds, along with black. While the fabrics range in value from light to dark, the blocks are not strictly divided into light and dark halves, as with most Log Cabin blocks. Rather, the light and dark fabrics are sprinkled across the surface of the quilt, giving it a more spontaneous feeling.

Don't worry about choosing fabrics that necessarily go together.

Quilt Sizes			
	Twin (shown)	Double	Queen
Finished Quilt Size	69½" × 87½"	83" × 101"	92" × 105½"
Finished Block Size	4½"	4½"	4½"
Number of Blocks	221	320	378

Materials			
	Twin	Double	Queen
Assorted solids	10⅛ yards	14½ yards	17⅛ yards
Black	1¼ yards	1⅜ yards	1⅜ yards
Backing	5½ yards	7⅞ yards	8⅜ yards
Batting (optional)	76" × 94"	90" × 108"	98" × 112"
Binding	⅝ yard	¾ yard	¾ yard
Foundation material	4½ yards	5⅝ yards	6⅜ yards

NOTE: Yardages are based on 44/45-inch-wide fabrics that are at least 42 inches wide after preshrinking.

Instead, select groups of solids based on their light, medium, and dark values. See page 120 in "Log Cabin Basics" for a detailed discussion of color and value.

The yardage requirements are generous estimates of the amounts actually used in the quilt. For a successful scrap quilt, variety is important, so you will likely start out with more yardage than indi-cated, but not all of it will be used. In addition to the pieced outer border, there are four narrow inner borders: two are black, one is pieced, and one is made from one of the fabrics used in the blocks. Decide on a color for this fourth border, and make sure you have at least ½ yard of it on hand—more if you also wish to use it extensively in the blocks.

Cutting Chart			
Fabric	Strip Width	Number of Strips	
		Twin	Double	Queen
Assorted solids	1¼"	308	404	479
Border 4 fabric	1"	7	9	10
Black	1"	43	53	57

To help develop your own unique color scheme for the quilt, photocopy the **Color Plan** on page 43, and use crayons or colored pencils to experiment with different color arrangements.

CUTTING

Referring to the Cutting Chart, cut the strips and borders needed for which quilt size you are making. Measurements for the borders include ¼-inch seam allowances. Cut all strips across the fabric width (crosswise grain). **Note:** Cut and piece one sample block before cutting all the pieces for the quilt.

The pieces in the block have a finished width of ½ inch. If you were piecing traditionally, you would cut 1-inch-wide strips. For the foundation method, begin by cutting 1¼-inch-wide strips from the fabrics. You may wish to decrease that width in ⅛-inch increments as you become more familiar with the technique, but don't cut pieces less than 1 inch wide.

The number of strips needed for logs is estimated based on using full-width yardage. If you are using scraps, the number of strips needed will vary.

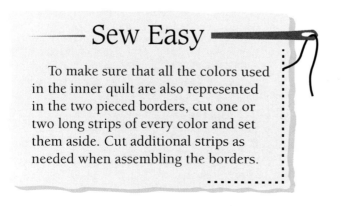

— Sew Easy

To make sure that all the colors used in the inner quilt are also represented in the two pieced borders, cut one or two long strips of every color and set them aside. Cut additional strips as needed when assembling the borders.

MAKING THE FOUNDATIONS

Step 1. Make a template by enlarging the block pattern on page 42. Make a second template by tracing the full-size corner block on page 42.

Step 2. Following the instructions on page 123 in "Log Cabin Basics," transfer the pattern to your chosen foundation material. Make sure the marked lines are visible from the back side when you hold the foundation up to the light. Use the **Block Diagrams** as a reference for piecing order. Cut out the foundations, leaving a bit of extra material on all sides. Set the corner block foundations aside for now.

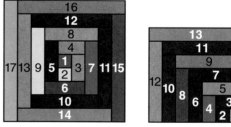

Corner Block

Block Diagrams

PIECING THE BLOCKS

Make a sample block before cutting fabric for the entire quilt. If you experience problems while assembling the block, increase the strip width. Using strips slightly wider than necessary can be a real time-saver since not as much precision is required when positioning them for sewing. Reevaluate your work often. You may find that strip width can be decreased again once you are more familiar with the method.

Sew Easy

If you have chosen to use the chain-piecing method without a foundation, you'll need to cut the logs to length before sewing them. Refer to the list below to cut the strips into logs. The dimensions include ¼-inch seam allowances.

Log Number	Log Size
1, 2	1" × 1"
3, 4	1" × 1½"
5, 6	1" × 2"
7, 8	1" × 2½"
9, 10	1" × 3"
11, 12	1" × 3½"
13, 14	1" × 4"
15, 16	1" × 4½"
17	1" × 5"

The blocks in this quilt are not all clearly divided into dark and light halves. For best results, cut several strips of fabric in different colors and values and use them randomly to piece the sample block.

Step 1. Cut a 1¼-inch square of fabric for the block center, and place it right side up on the back side of a foundation, covering the area of piece 1, as shown in **Diagram 1**. Secure with tape, a bit of glue, or a pin. Hold the foundation up to the light with the back side away from you. You should be able to see a shadow of the square through the foundation. Check to make sure it extends past all lines surrounding piece 1.

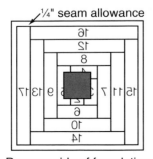

Reverse side of foundation

Diagram 1

Step 2. Select a strip of fabric for piece 2 and position it right side down on piece 1, as shown in **Diagram 2A**. Holding the fabric in position, flip the foundation to its front side and sew on the line separating pieces 1 and 2, as shown in **2B**. Begin and end the line of stitches approximately ⅛ inch on either side of the line.

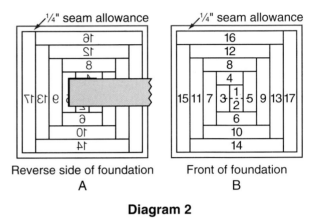

Reverse side of foundation
A

Front of foundation
B

Diagram 2

Step 3. Remove the foundation from the machine and flip it to the back side. If you used tape to secure the center piece, remove it now. Cut away the excess tail of fabric (cut just past the end of stitches, as shown in **Diagram 3A**). Flip piece 2 into a right-side-up position, finger pressing it into place. See **3B**.

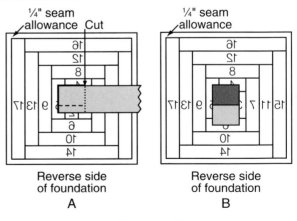

Reverse side
of foundation
A

Reverse side
of foundation
B

Diagram 3

Step 4. Position the next strip right side down, as shown in **Diagram 4A** on page 38. Holding the strip in place, turn the foundation over and sew on the vertical line separating pieces 1 and 2 from piece 3, again beginning and ending approximately ⅛ inch on either side of the line. Remove from the machine, trim the tail, and flip piece 3 into a right-side-up position, finger pressing it into place, as shown in **4B.** Check to make sure all unsewn edges of piece 3 overlap seam lines around the piece's border.

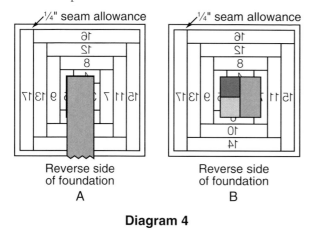

Diagram 4

Step 5. Continue to add pieces in numerical order. Remember to trim excess bulk from seam allowances, finger press each piece into place, and check to make sure the new piece overlaps all unsewn seam lines before stitching the next strip. After you have added the last piece, press with a warm iron, then cut on the outer line of the seam allowance.

ASSEMBLING THE QUILT TOP

Step 1. Use a design wall or flat surface to lay out your blocks, rearranging them as necessary until you are satisfied with the color placement. Use the photo on page 34, the **Twin-Size Quilt Diagram,** or your own shaded drawing as a guide to block placement. Don't hesitate to flip blocks upside down or side to side if doing so improves the overall look of your quilt. As illustrated in **Diagram 5,** the blocks in the quilt shown don't all share the same orientation.

The **Twin-Size Quilt Diagram** illustrates the layout of the twin-size quilt, which has 17 rows of

13 blocks each. The layout for the other two quilts is essentially the same: The double is made up of 20 rows with 16 blocks in each, and the queen size has 21 rows with 18 blocks in each.

Step 2. When you are satisfied with the layout, sew your blocks into rows, pressing the seams in opposite directions from row to row. If you are using removable foundations, tear away the portion surrounding the seam allowances where blocks were joined.

Note: Permanent foundations create additional bulk in the seam allowance. If seams are too bulky to press to one side, it may be necessary to press them open. Be sure to match and pin pressed-open seams carefully when rows are joined.

Step 3. Sew the rows together, carefully matching seams. Tear away all remaining portions of removable foundations. Press the seam allowances where rows were joined.

MAKING AND ADDING THE NARROW BORDERS

This quilt has four narrow borders, each with a finished width of ½ inch. The first border is plain, the second is pieced, and the third and fourth are plain. There is also a wider pieced border that finishes at 3½ inches. **Diagram 6** is a detail of one corner of the quilt, showing how the borders and corner blocks work together.

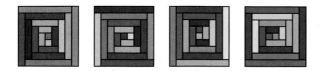

Diagram 5

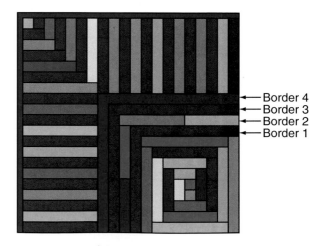

Diagram 6

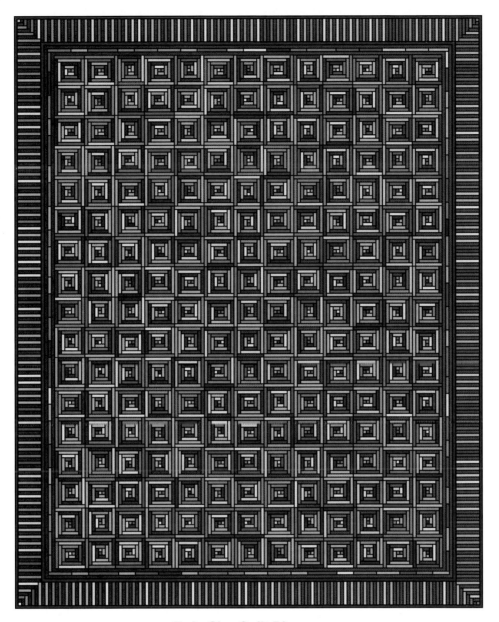

Twin-Size Quilt Diagram

Step 1. To make the three plain borders long enough, the 1-inch-wide strips must be sewn together end to end. Make all the side borders and all the top and bottom borders the same length to begin with, then trim them to the exact length later. For the twin-size quilt, sew two strips together for each side border, and sew one and a half strips together for each top and bottom border. For the double quilt, sew two and a half strips together for each side border, and sew two strips together for each top and bottom border. For the queen-size quilt, sew two and a half strips together for each of the four borders.

Step 2. To add the first border, measure the quilt from top to bottom, taking the measurement through the vertical center of the quilt, not at the sides. Cut two of the black side border strips to this length.

Step 3. Fold one strip in half crosswise and crease. Unfold it and position it right side down along one side of the quilt top, with the crease at the horizontal midpoint. Pin at the midpoint and ends first, then along the length of the entire side, easing in fullness if necessary. Sew the border to the quilt using a ¼-inch seam allowance.

Step 4. Repeat on the opposite side of the quilt.

Step 5. Measure the quilt from side to side, taking the measurement through the horizontal center of the quilt, not at the sides. Trim two of the black top and bottom border strips to this length. Add them to the quilt in the same manner as for the side borders.

Step 6. The next border is pieced from 1-inch-wide segments of various lengths cut from the same fabrics used in the blocks. Gather together all log segments left over from assembling the blocks. If necessary, trim them to 1 inch wide. Without sewing them together yet, arrange the segments into four long strips. As a general guideline for figuring the length of the strips, add 1 or 2 inches to the measurements you took for the first border. You will cut the strips to the exact length later. Cut additional 1-inch-wide segments if necessary, varying their length and color to create a pleasing design. As you lay out the segments, overlap the ends by ¼ inch to compensate for seam allowances. When you are pleased with the appearance, begin sewing the segments together end to end, as shown in **Diagram 7.** Continue sewing until the strip length is slightly longer than required. Press the seams in one direction.

Diagram 7

Step 7. Measure and add the pieced border to the quilt top in the same manner as the black border, trimming each strip to the exact length required before sewing it to the quilt top.

Step 8. The third and fourth borders are plain and are added in the same manner as the first narrow black border. Use black strips for the third border and strips from one of the other colors for the fourth border. (The remaining black strips will be used in the pieced outer border.) Measure and trim the strips to length, and add them to the quilt sides first, then to the top and bottom.

— Sew Easy —

If color placement is not critical, the border strips can be strip pieced, then cut apart. Sew segments of varying lengths together end to end as described in Steps 6 and 7, but change the segment width to 2½ inches (the extra ½ inch will allow you to square up the strip if necessary). Make a 2½-inch-wide strip of calculated length (plus a bit extra) for side borders and another for top and bottom borders. After pressing, cut two 1-inch-wide strips from each pieced unit. Be sure to square up one side of the pieced unit before cutting the strips. Measure and trim each side strip to correct length. Flip the strips in opposite directions before sewing them to the quilt. Repeat for the top and bottom borders.

The same technique can be used to piece the wide outer borders. Cut the strips so they measure 1 × 8½ inches, and sew them together along the long edges. Make a strip set for the side borders and one for the top and bottom borders. After sewing the strips together and pressing them, square up one edge of each segment, then cut two 4-inch-wide pieces from each.

MAKING AND ADDING THE WIDE BORDER

The wide outer border is pieced from 1 × 4-inch strips of solid-color fabrics alternating with black. The alternating color scheme is continued in the corner blocks, giving the corners a mitered appearance.

Step 1. Measure the side border length as you did for the narrow borders. Divide the length by ½ inch, the finished size of each strip, and subtract 1 to allow for the seam allowance at each end. The result is the number of strips needed for the side border. For example, the side border on the twin quilt should measure approximately 81 inches. Divide by $\frac{1}{2}$ (0.5) to get 162, then subtract 1. You will need 161 strips for each side border. If the actual length is not evenly divisible by $\frac{1}{2}$, it may be necessary to ease in fullness as you pin the border to the sides of quilt.

Each border on the quilt shown begins and ends with a black strip. If you choose to follow the same layout, it may again be necessary to ease in fullness as you sew since actual seam allowances vary from quilter to quilter.

Step 2. Cut the black and color strips into $1 \times 4\frac{1}{4}$-inch segments. (The extra $\frac{1}{4}$ inch allows for slight inaccuracies in aligning strips.) Lay out the strips, rearranging them until you are satisfied with the color placement. Sew the strips together, as shown in **Diagram 8**. Be very careful to match the strips exactly. Press all seams in the same direction. Measure the strip to be sure length is correct, then trim it to the correct 4-inch width. Make a second side border the same way.

Diagram 8

Step 3. Measure for the top and bottom borders now, before sewing the side borders to the quilt, and piece the top and bottom borders in the same way you did the side borders.

Step 4. Sew a pieced border to one side of the quilt, using the same method as for the narrow borders. Repeat on the opposite side.

Step 5. Referring to the **Block Diagrams** on page 36, make four corner blocks using the foundations prepared earlier.

Step 6. Sew a block to each end of the top and bottom borders, positioning the blocks so that piece 1 is always at the outermost corner of the quilt. Refer to the photo on page 34 and the **Twin-Size Quilt Diagram** on page 39 for correct positioning. Sew the top and bottom borders to the quilt.

QUILTING AND FINISHING

Step 1. Mark the quilt top for quilting, if desired. The quilt shown is quilted along each seam line.

Step 2. Regardless of which quilt size you've chosen to make, the backing will have to be pieced. To make the most efficient use of the backing yardage, piece the back for the double and queen-size quilts with the seams running horizontally across the quilt. For the twin-size quilt, piece the back with the seams running vertically. **Diagram 9** illustrates the three quilt backs. Begin by trimming the selvages from the fabric.

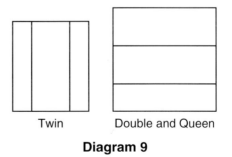

Twin   Double and Queen

Diagram 9

Step 3. For the twin-size quilt, divide the fabric crosswise into two equal pieces. Divide one of the pieces in half lengthwise, and sew one half to each side of the full-width piece. Press the seams open.

Step 4. For the double quilt, the backing should measure approximately 95×113 inches. Divide the yardage crosswise into three equal pieces, and sew two of the pieces together along the long edge. Measure the width of the joined pieces, and subtract the result from 113. This is the width of the strip you must cut from the third piece of fabric. Add the strip to the joined piece and press the seam open.

Step 5. For the queen-size quilt, the backing should measure approximately 104 × 118 inches. Divide the yardage crosswise into three equal pieces, and sew two of the pieces together along the long edge. Measure the width of the joined pieces, and subtract the result from 118 to find the width of the strip that must be cut from the remaining piece. Sew the strip to the joined piece and press the seam open.

Step 6. Layer the backing, batting if used, and quilt top, and baste. Quilt as desired.

Step 7. Referring to the directions on page 137 in "Quiltmaking Basics," make and attach double-fold binding. To calculate the amount of binding needed for the quilt size you are making, add up the length of the four sides of the quilt and add 9 inches. The total is the approximate number of inches of binding you will need.

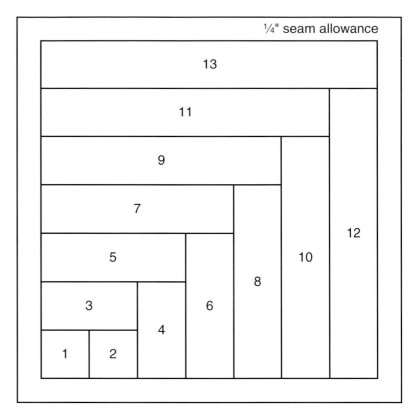

Corner Block Pattern

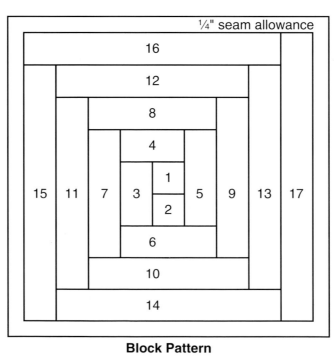

Block Pattern

Pattern shown is the mirror image of the finished block.
Note: Pattern is reduced. Enlarge it 150 percent before tracing.

Nineteenth-Century Amish Log Cabin
Color Plan

Photocopy this page and use it to experiment with color schemes for your quilt.
To maximize the space for coloring, only the left half of the quilt is shown.
Make two photocopies and tape them together to complete the quilt.

43

PATHS TO THE DIAMONDS
Skill Level: *Easy*

*U*nlike the more common scrap Log Cabins, this contemporary interpretation of the traditional Barn Raising setting relies on a particular color scheme for its effect. Subtle tones of gray work well with the white and black prints to create a bold overall design. This large wallhanging was inspired by a lecture given by author and quiltmaker Mary Ellen Hopkins.

BEFORE YOU BEGIN

The directions for this quilt are written based on using the chain-piecing technique, although the foundation method would work equally well. Read through the general construction directions in "Log Cabin Basics," beginning on page 118, to become familiar with the technique. All of the logs are cut to length, then the blocks are pieced in assembly line fashion. If you prefer to use the foundation method, prepare a foundation for each block using the pattern on page 51.

CHOOSING FABRICS

The blocks in this quilt are divided into two color schemes. While the red centers and the three light prints are the same in all 64 blocks, in half the blocks they are combined with gray prints and in the other half with black prints. For best results, select prints that vary in scale and texture. In the quilt shown, the same large-scale black-and-red floral was used in two places in the blocks, as well as in the border.

If you wish to develop your own unique color scheme, photocopy the **Color Plan** on page 50, and use crayons or colored pencils to experiment with different color arrangements.

Quilt Size

Finished Size	73½" × 73½"
Finished Block Size	8"
Number of Blocks	64

NOTE: Because specific color and value placement is critical to the overall design of this quilt, no variations in size or layout are provided.

Materials

Fabric	Amount
Red	1 yard
Light print 1	¾ yard
Light print 2	1 yard
Light print 3	1¼ yards
Black print 1	2 yards
Black print 2	¾ yard
Medium gray print 1	⅝ yard
Medium gray print 2	⅝ yard
Dark gray print	⅞ yard
Backing	4¾ yards
Batting	80" × 80"
Binding	⅝ yard

NOTE: Yardages are based on 44/45-inch-wide fabrics that are at least 42 inches wide after preshrinking.

Cutting Chart

Fabric	Strip Width	Number of Strips	Piece	Log Length	Number Needed
Red	1½"	8	Border		
	2½"	4	Log 1	2½"	64
Light print 1	1½"	10	Log 2	2½"	64
			Log 3	3½"	64
Light print 2	1½"	18	Log 6	4½"	64
			Log 7	5½"	64
Light print 3	1½"	24	Log 10	6½"	64
			Log 11	7½"	64
Black print 1	4"	8	Border		
	1½"	21	Log 4	3½"	32
			Log 5	4½"	32
			Log 12	7½"	32
			Log 13	8½"	32
Black print 2	1½"	11	Log 8	5½"	32
			Log 9	6½"	32
Medium gray print 1	1½"	7	Log 4	3½"	32
			Log 5	4½"	32
Medium gray print 2	1½"	11	Log 8	5½"	32
			Log 9	6½"	32
Dark gray print	1½"	14	Log 12	7½"	32
			Log 13	8½"	32

CUTTING

All measurements include ¼-inch seam allowances. Referring to the Cutting Chart, cut strips in the width needed, then cut the strips into logs. Cut all strips across the fabric width (crosswise grain). You may find it helpful to pin a number label to each group of logs as you cut them. **Note:** Cut and piece one sample block before cutting all the pieces for the quilt.

PIECING THE FIRST BLOCK

Refer to "Log Cabin Basics," beginning on page 118, and read through the directions for the technique you have chosen. Piece a sample block first;

it will allow you to become acquainted with the technique and to double-check the accuracy of your seam allowances. Cut enough light print and either gray print or black print logs for one block, and use the **Block Diagram** as a color sample and a guide for piecing order. The completed block should measure 8½ inches square.

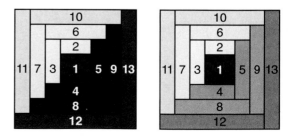

Block Diagram

── Sew Easy ──

It's important to press each log before adding the next. Pressing opens up the seam, "stretching" a log to its full width. Always press the seam allowance toward the log you have just added.

Step 1. Place a light print log 2 right sides together with a red log 1, aligning the edges. Stitch the pieces together using a ¼-inch seam. Open out the pieces, as shown in **Diagram 1A**, and press the seam allowance toward log 2.

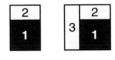

Diagram 1

Step 2. Referring to **Diagram 1B**, position log 3 right sides together with the pieced segment, and stitch. Press the seam allowance toward log 3.

Step 3. Add log 4 to the bottom of the pieced segment, as shown in **Diagram 2A**. Press the seam toward log 4.

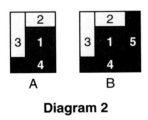

Diagram 2

Step 4. In the same manner, sew log 5 to the side of the pieced segment, as shown in **2B**. Press the seam allowance toward log 5.

Step 5. Continue to add logs in numerical order in a counterclockwise direction until all 13 logs have been added. Measure your completed block to make sure it is an accurate 8½ inches square. If it isn't, check your seam allowances and make any necessary adjustments.

PIECING THE REMAINING BLOCKS

Chain piecing can help speed up the block assembly process. Instead of making an individual block from start to finish, perform one step at a time on all blocks of the same color scheme.

Step 1. Stack the light print logs and the gray print logs near your sewing machine. Keep your sample block handy to use as a color guide. Stitch a log 2 to a red log 1 as described previously. Without removing the stitched pair from the sewing machine and without lifting the presser foot, insert and sew a second pair. Continue sewing until all remaining center sections are pieced. See **Diagram 3**.

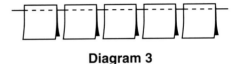

Diagram 3

Step 2. Cut the stitched segments apart. Press each seam allowance toward log 2. In the same manner, add the remaining logs to the blocks until you have completed all 32 gray print blocks.

Step 3. Repeat the process for the 32 black print blocks.

ASSEMBLING THE QUILT TOP

Step 1. The blocks are arranged in eight rows, with eight blocks in each row. Use a design wall or flat surface to arrange your blocks, as shown in **Diagram 4** on page 48.

······· Sew Quick ·······

It may not be necessary to pin short logs to the block as you sew, especially if you are using 100 percent cottons, which "stick" to each other nicely. As you begin adding longer logs, secure their edges with a few straight pins to help keep your piecing accurate.

Row 1

Row 2

Row 3

Row 4

Row 5

Row 6

Row 7

Row 8

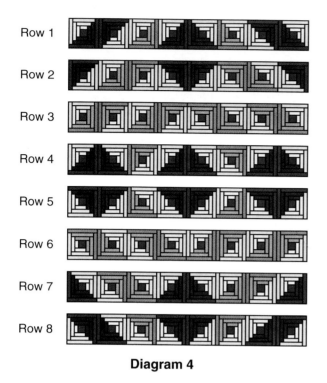

Diagram 4

Step 2. Sew the blocks into rows, pressing the seam allowances in opposite directions from row to row.

Step 3. Sew the rows together, carefully matching seams where blocks meet. If you've pressed the seam allowances in opposite directions, the seams should fit tightly against each other, helping you achieve a perfect match. Press seam allowances where rows were joined.

ADDING THE BORDERS

Step 1. Sew the 1½-inch-wide red border strips together in pairs, making four long borders.

Step 2. Measure the length of the quilt top, taking the measurement through the vertical center of the quilt rather than along the sides. Cut two of the long red border strips to this length.

Step 3. Fold one strip in half crosswise and crease. Unfold it and position it right side down along one side of the quilt top, with the crease at the horizontal midpoint. Pin at the midpoint and ends first, then along the length of the entire side, easing in fullness if necessary. Sew the border to the quilt top using a ¼-inch seam allowance. Repeat on the opposite side of the quilt.

Step 4. Measure the width of the quilt, taking the measurement through the horizontal center of the quilt and including the side borders. Cut the remaining two red border strips to this length.

Step 5. Fold one strip in half crosswise and crease. Unfold it and position it right side down along one end of the quilt top, matching the crease to the vertical midpoint. Pin at the midpoint and ends first, then across the entire width of the quilt top, easing in fullness if necessary. Stitch, using a ¼-inch seam allowance. Repeat on the opposite end of the quilt top.

Step 6. Sew the 4-inch-wide black print border strips together in pairs, making four long border strips.

Step 7. In the same manner as for the red border, measure, cut, and sew the 4-inch-wide border strips to the quilt sides.

Step 8. Measure, cut, and sew the 4-inch-wide border strips to the quilt ends. The completed quilt top should look like the one shown in the **Quilt Diagram.**

QUILTING AND FINISHING

Step 1. Mark the quilt top for quilting. The angular lines of this quilt were softened by a quilting design of flowing fanlike curves that follow the contours of the dark diamond shapes. Segments of the motif are repeated in light areas, radiating outward from the center of the quilt.

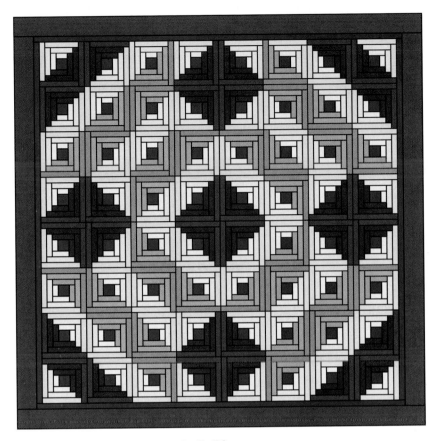

Quilt Diagram

Step 2. To piece the quilt back, first trim the selvages from the backing fabric. Cut the 4¾-yard piece of backing fabric into two equal segments, each 2⅜ yards long.

Step 3. Cut one of the segments in half vertically, producing two narrow segments that are each approximately 22 inches wide and 2⅜ yards long. Sew a narrow segment to each side of the uncut 2⅜-yard piece, as shown in **Diagram 5.** Press the seams open.

Step 4. Layer the quilt top, batting, and backing. Baste the layers together. Quilt as desired.

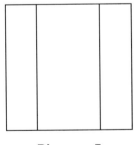

Diagram 5

Step 5. Make approximately 325 inches of double-fold binding. Refer to page 137 in "Quilt-making Basics" for complete directions on making and attaching binding.

PATHS TO THE DIAMONDS
Color Plan

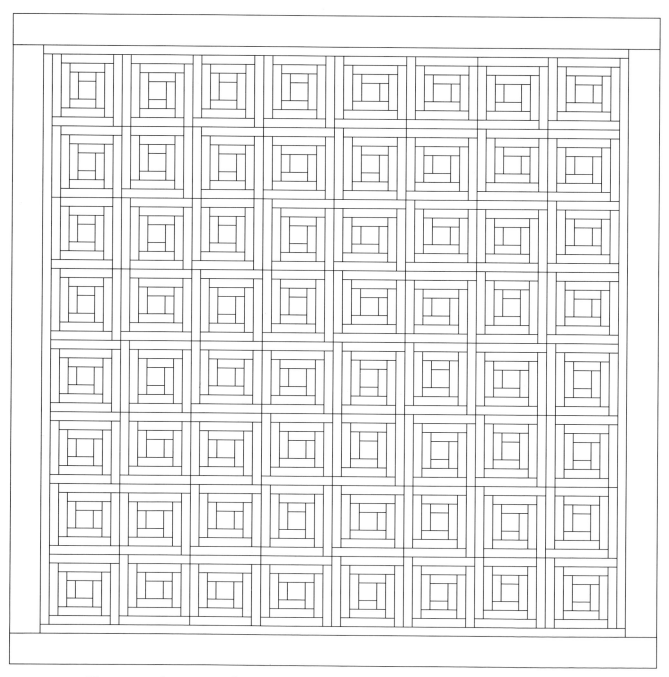

Photocopy this page and use it to experiment with color schemes for your quilt.

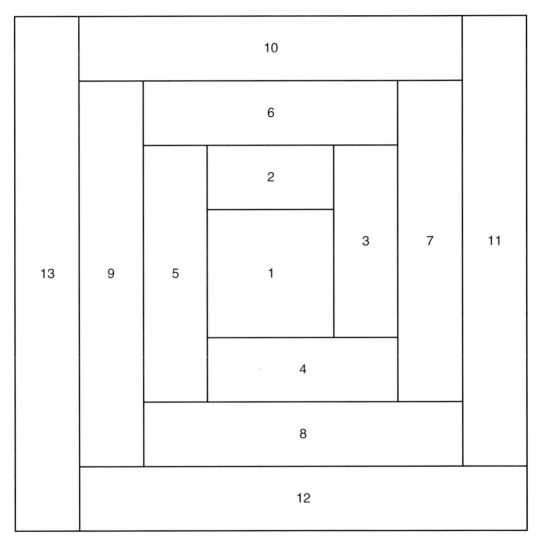

Block Pattern

Pattern shown is the mirror image of the finished block.
Note: Pattern is reduced. Enlarge it 150 percent before tracing.

BARN RAISING
Skill Level: *Easy*

B old, vibrant colors in a traditional setting make up this striking king-size quilt. The dramatic interplay of colors creates an almost three-dimensional effect, making it easy to imagine the beams of a new barn, which give the setting its name. Surprisingly subtle visual effects are created by six color variations of the basic block.

BEFORE YOU BEGIN

The directions for this quilt are written using the chain-piecing technique, although the foundation method would work equally well. Read through the general construction directions in "Log Cabin Basics," beginning on page 118, to become familiar with the technique. All of the logs are cut to length, then the blocks are pieced in assembly line fashion. If you prefer to use the foundation method, prepare a foundation for each block using the pattern on page 59. The pattern given is reduced in size and must be enlarged 150 percent before tracing. See page 132 in "Quilt-making Basics" for details on enlarging patterns.

CHOOSING FABRICS

Although at first glance this quilt appears to consist of simple half-light and half-dark blocks, it actually has a very complex, yet subtle, color arrangement. If you study the photo, you'll notice that the quiltmaker rearranged the placement of the fabrics to get six different color variations. **Diagram 1** on page 54 illustrates the six different blocks.

If you wish to create your own unique color scheme, photocopy the **Color Plan** on page 58, and use crayons or colored pencils to experiment with different color arrangements.

Note: There are actually two different medium purple fabrics used in the quilt, but they are so close in value that we have treated them as one

Quilt Size

Finished Quilt Size	115½" × 115½"
Finished Block Size	10"
Number of Blocks	100

NOTE: Because specific color and value placement is critical to the overall design of this quilt, no variations in size or layout are provided.

Materials

Fabric	Amount
Navy blue	5¼ yards
Royal blue	1¾ yards
Medium purple	2½ yards
Light teal	3 yards
Medium teal	1½ yards
Dark teal	1½ yards
Magenta	1½ yards
Rose pink	⅜ yard
Backing	10¼ yards
Batting	120" × 120"

NOTE: Yardages are based on 44/45-inch-wide fabrics that are at least 42 inches wide after preshrinking.

fabric in the Materials list and Cutting Chart. The same is true for the light teal. If you choose to purchase two different fabrics in each color, make sure they are similar in color and value.

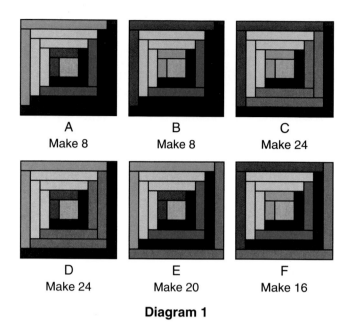

A
Make 8

B
Make 8

C
Make 24

D
Make 24

E
Make 20

F
Make 16

Diagram 1

CUTTING

All measurements include ¼-inch seam allowances. Referring to the Cutting Chart, cut strips in the width needed, then cut the strips into logs. Cut all strips across the fabric width (crosswise grain). You may find it helpful to pin a number label to each group of logs as you cut them. **Note:** Cut and piece one block before cutting all the pieces for the quilt.

PIECING THE FIRST BLOCK

Refer to "Log Cabin Basics," beginning on page 118, and read through the directions for the tech-

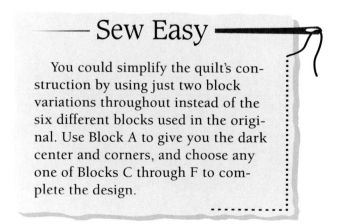

— Sew Easy —

You could simplify the quilt's construction by using just two block variations throughout instead of the six different blocks used in the original. Use Block A to give you the dark center and corners, and choose any one of Blocks C through F to complete the design.

nique you have chosen. Piece a sample block first; it will allow you to become acquainted with the technique and to double-check the accuracy of your seam allowances. Cut enough logs for one sample block, and use the **Block Diagram** and the **Fabric Key** as guides to piecing order.

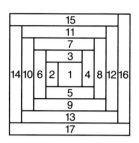

Block Diagram

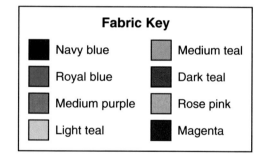

Fabric Key

■	Navy blue	▨	Medium teal
■	Royal blue	■	Dark teal
■	Medium purple	▨	Rose pink
▨	Light teal	■	Magenta

Step 1. Place a log 2 right sides together with a center piece 1, aligning the edges. Stitch the pieces together using a ¼-inch seam. Open out the pieces, as shown in **Diagram 2A**, and press the seam allowance toward log 2. Always press the seam allowance toward the log you have just added.

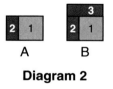

A   B

Diagram 2

Step 2. Place a log 3 right sides together with the pieced segment, aligning the edges. Stitch the pieces together. Open out the pieces and press the seam allowance toward log 3. See **2B**.

Step 3. Sew a log 4 to the right side of the pieced segment, as shown in **Diagram 3A**, and

Cutting Chart

Fabric	Strip Width	Number of Strips	Piece	Length	Number Needed
Navy blue	5½"	11	Border		
	1½"	74	4	3½"	100
			5	4½"	100
			12	7½"	52
			13	8½"	52
			16	9½"	64
			17	10½"	64
Royal blue	2½"	10	Border		
	1½"	17	8	5½"	52
			9	6½"	52
Medium purple	1½"	53	8	5½"	48
			9	6½"	48
			12	7½"	48
			13	8½"	48
			16	9½"	36
			17	10½"	100
Light teal	1½"	65	6	4½"	100
			7	5½"	100
			10	6½"	100
			11	7½"	100
Medium teal	1½"	31	2	2½"	48
			3	3½"	48
			14	8½"	52
			15	9½"	52
Dark teal	1½"	31	2	2½"	52
			3	3½"	52
			14	8½"	48
			15	9½"	48
Rose pink	2½"	6	1	2½"	100

press. Sew a log 5 to the bottom of the segment and press. See **3B.**

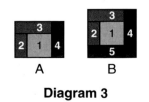

Diagram 3

Step 4. Continue to add logs in numerical order until all 17 logs have been added. The completed block should measure 10½ inches square. If it does, you have established an accurate ¼-inch seam allowance and are pressing seams carefully. If the block measures a different size, double-check your seam allowances. If you need more practice, make another sample block before continuing.

PIECING THE REMAINING BLOCKS

Chain piecing can help speed up the block assembly process. Instead of making an individual block from start to finish, perform one step at a time on all the blocks. The easiest way to organize your sewing for this quilt is to make all the blocks for variation A, then move on to variation B, and so on.

Step 1. Cut and stack all the logs for block variation A, placing them in numerical order near your sewing machine. Stitch a log 2 to a center piece 1 as described previously. Without removing the stitched pair from the sewing machine, feed a second pair under the presser foot and sew them together. Continue sewing until all remaining center sections are pieced. See **Diagram 4.**

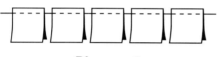

Diagram 4

Step 2. Cut the stitched segments apart. Press each seam allowance toward log 2.

Step 3. In the same manner, add log 3 to all of the blocks. Cut the segments apart and press each seam allowance toward log 3. Continue adding logs in numerical order until all of the variation A blocks are completed.

Step 4. Repeat Steps 1 through 3 for the five remaining block variations, completing each type before moving on to the next.

ASSEMBLING THE QUILT TOP

Step 1. The blocks are arranged in ten rows, each containing ten blocks. Referring to **Diagram 5,** the **Quilt Diagram,** and the photo on page 52, carefully lay out the blocks. **Diagram 5** shows the correct placement of the blocks in the layout, while the **Quilt Diagram** and the photo illustrate the correct orientation. Check to make sure the blocks are turned the right way.

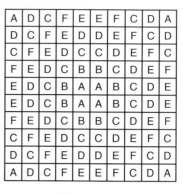

A	D	C	F	E	E	F	C	D	A
D	C	F	E	D	D	E	F	C	D
C	F	E	D	C	C	D	E	F	C
F	E	D	C	B	B	C	D	E	F
E	D	C	B	A	A	B	C	D	E
E	D	C	B	A	A	B	C	D	E
F	E	D	C	B	B	C	D	E	F
C	F	E	D	C	C	D	E	F	C
D	C	F	E	D	D	E	F	C	D
A	D	C	F	E	E	F	C	D	A

Diagram 5

Step 2. Sew the blocks into rows, pressing the seam allowances in opposite directions from row to row.

Step 3. Join the rows, carefully matching seams where blocks meet. If you pressed the seams in opposite directions, the seams should fit tightly against each other, helping you to achieve a perfect match. Press seam allowances where rows are joined.

ADDING THE BORDERS

Step 1. To make the narrow inner border, sew eight of the 2½-inch-wide royal blue strips together in pairs. Cut the remaining two strips in half, and sew one half to each of the four long strips.

Step 2. Measure the quilt from top to bottom, taking the measurement through the vertical center of the quilt, not at the sides. Cut two of the long strips to this length.

Step 3. Fold one strip in half crosswise and crease. Unfold it and position it right side down along one edge of the quilt top, with the crease at the horizontal midpoint. Pin at the midpoint and ends first, then along the length of the entire side, easing in fullness if necessary. Sew the border to the quilt top using a ¼-inch seam allowance. Press the seam allowance toward the border. Repeat on the opposite side.

Step 4. Measure the width of the quilt, taking the measurement through the horizontal center of

Quilt Diagram

the quilt and including the side borders. Cut the remaining two royal blue strips to this length.

Step 5. In the same manner as for the side borders, position and pin a strip along one end of the quilt top, easing in fullness if necessary. Stitch, using a ¼-inch seam allowance. Press the seam toward the border. Repeat on the opposite end.

Step 6. Use the 5½-inch-wide navy blue strips for the wide outer border. The side borders consist of two and a half strips each, while the top and bottom borders consist of three strips each. Add the borders to the quilt top in the same manner as for the inner borders.

QUILTING AND FINISHING

Step 1. Mark the quilt top for quilting. The quilt shown was quilted with diagonal lines in the inner border and garlands of hearts in the outer border. The blocks are quilted in the ditch.

Step 2. The backing should be approximately 125 inches square. Cut the 10¾-yard piece of backing fabric into three equal segments, and trim the selvages. Sew the panels together lengthwise and press the seams open.

Step 3. Layer the backing, batting, and quilt top; baste the layers together. Quilt as desired.

Step 4. Referring to the directions on page 137 in "Quiltmaking Basics," use the magenta fabric to make double-fold binding. The quilt shown is finished with ¾-inch-wide binding. If you wish to make your binding this wide, cut the binding strips 4½ inches wide, and attach the binding to the quilt using a ¾-inch seam. You will need approximately 475 inches of binding.

BARN RAISING

Color Plan

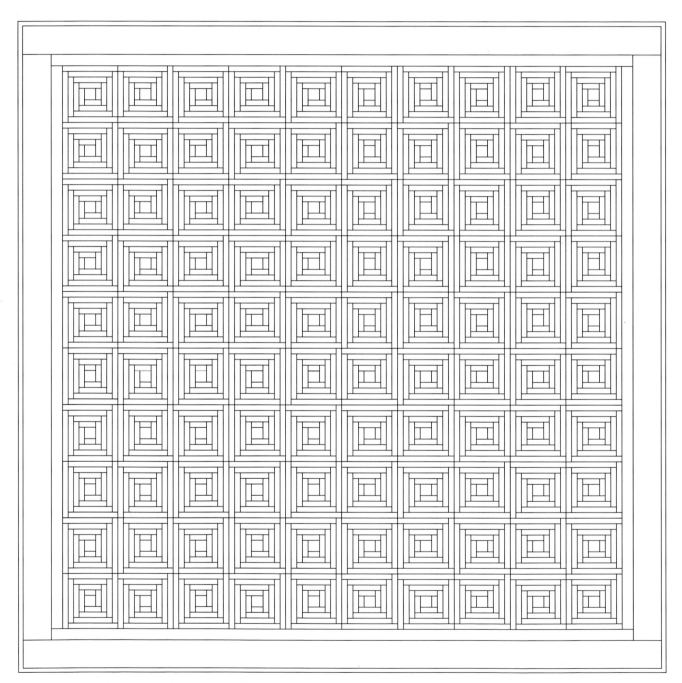

Photocopy this page and use it to experiment with color schemes for your quilt.

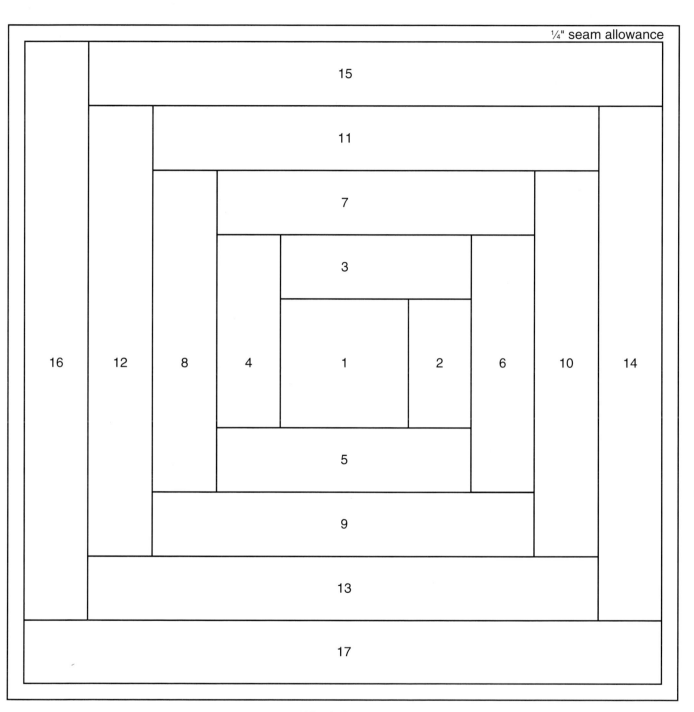

Block Pattern

Pattern shown is the mirror image of the finished block.
Note: Pattern is reduced. Enlarge it 150 percent before tracing.

COURTHOUSE STEPS

Skill Level: *Easy*

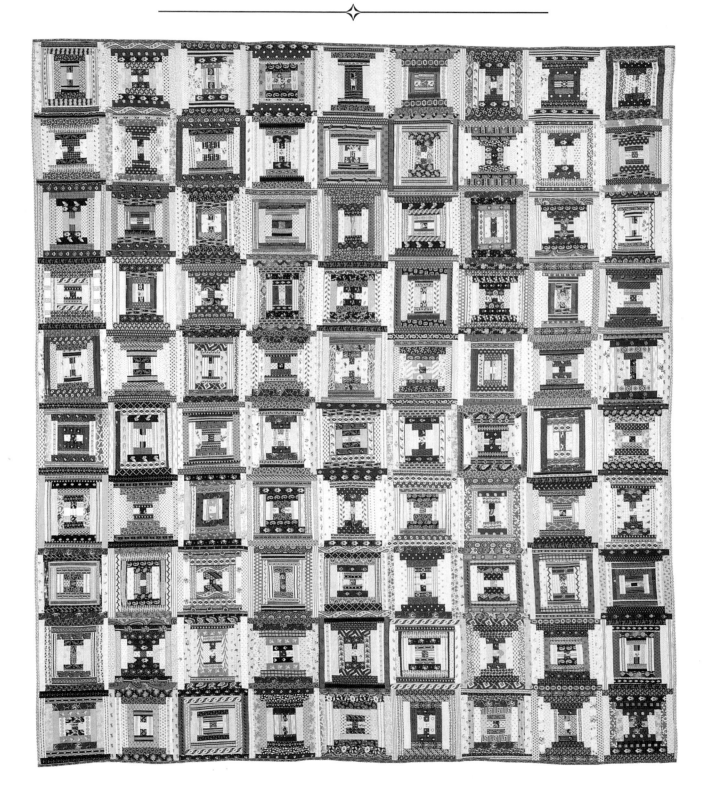

*I*f quilts could talk, this one would surely have a story to tell! This beautifully preserved double quilt was stitched by Anne Fryer Bedford, who was born in 1797 and began the quilt in her school days. The records show that Anne was married in 1820, raised six children, and somehow managed to keep this quilt with her and keep working on it throughout most of her life. The quilt was apparently finished sometime after 1860, since the binding was added by machine.

BEFORE YOU BEGIN

The directions for this quilt are written based on using the foundation method, which is the technique used in the original quilt, although the chain-piecing method could also be used. Read through the general construction directions in "Log Cabin Basics," beginning on page 118, to become familiar with the foundation technique. Prepare a foundation for each block using the full-size pattern on page 67. One-half of the pattern is given; trace two halves and carefully join them to make the complete template. If you prefer to use the chain-piecing technique, see page 121 for details.

There are two versions of the Log Cabin block, the only difference being the placement of the lights and darks. The light blocks begin with a light center, the dark ones with a dark center. Each block then alternates the lights and darks outward from the center. When set together, the dark blocks are turned 90 degress (a quarter turn) clockwise to create the diamond pattern.

Quilt Sizes			
	Crib	Double (shown)	Queen
Finished Quilt Size	41¼" × 57¾"	74¼" × 82½"	82½" × 99"
Finished Block Size	8¼"	8¼"	8¼"
Number of Full Blocks	35	90	120

Materials			
	Crib	Double	Queen
Dark fabrics	2 yards	5¼ yards	7 yards
Light fabrics	2 yards	5¼ yards	7 yards
Backing	2¾ yards	5¼ yards	7½ yards
Batting (optional)	47" × 64"	80" × 89"	89" × 105"
Binding	½ yard	⅝ yard	¾ yard
Foundation material	2¾ yards	5¼ yards	7 yards

NOTE: *Yardages are based on 44/45-inch-wide fabrics that are at least 42 inches wide after preshrinking.*

CHOOSING FABRICS

This Courthouse Steps design is made from a wide variety of fabrics of two basic values. To determine fabric placement, take a close look at the photo, the **Block Diagram** on page 62, and the **Double-Size Quilt Diagram** on page 65. For a discussion of color value, refer to page 120 in "Log Cabin Basics."

Choose print, stripe, and plaid

fabrics, and even solids to re-create the scrappy look of this quilt. The occasional brightly colored scrap, in this case blue or green, livens up a monochromatic color scheme.

To help develop your own unique color scheme for the quilt, photocopy the **Color Plan** on page 66, and use crayons or colored pencils to experiment with different color arrangements.

Light and dark yardages shown for blocks are generous estimates of the total yardage actually used in the quilt. Since small amounts of many fabrics are a key ingredient for a successful scrap quilt, you will likely begin with more yardage than indicated, but not all of it will be used.

CUTTING

Referring to the Cutting Chart, cut the number of strips needed. Cut all strips across the fabric width (crosswise grain). **Note:** Cut and sew one sample block before cutting all the pieces for the quilt.

All pieces in the Courthouse Steps block have a finished width of ¾ inch. If you were piecing traditionally, you would cut 1¼-inch-wide strips. For the foundation method, begin by cutting 1½-inch strips. You may wish to decrease that width in ⅛-inch increments as you become more familiar with the technique, but don't cut pieces less than 1¼ inches wide.

The number of dark and light strips needed for logs is estimated based on using full-width yardage. If you are using scraps, the number of strips needed will vary.

Cutting Chart

Fabric	Strip Width	Number of Strips		
		Crib	Double	Queen
Dark prints	1½"	53	135	180
Light prints	1½"	53	135	180

MAKING THE FOUNDATIONS

Step 1. One-half of the pattern for the Courthouse Steps block is given full size on page 67. Trace two halves of the pattern and carefully align the halves to create a template of the complete block, as shown in **Diagram 1**.

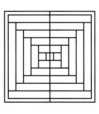

Diagram 1

Step 2. Following the instructions on page 123 in "Log Cabin Basics," transfer the pattern to your chosen foundation material. Use the **Block Diagram** as a color sample and a reference for piecing order. Cut out the foundations, leaving a bit of extra material on all sides.

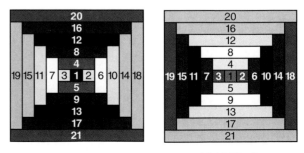

Dark Block   Light Block

Block Diagram

— Sew Easy —

If you have chosen to use the chain-piecing method without a foundation, you'll need to cut 1¼-inch-wide logs to length before sewing them. Refer to the list below to cut the strips into logs.

Log Number	Log Length
1, 2, 3	1¼"
4, 5, 6, 7	2¾"
8, 9, 10, 11	4¼"
12, 13, 14, 15	5¾"
16, 17, 18, 19	7¼"
20, 21	8¾"

PIECING THE BLOCKS

Make a sample block before cutting fabric for the entire quilt. If you experience problems while assembling the block, increase the strip width.

Step 1. Place a strip of dark fabric right side up on the back side of a foundation, covering the area of piece 1, as shown in **Diagram 2.** Secure with tape, a bit of glue stick, or a pin.

Hold the foundation up to the light with the back side away from you. You should be able to see a shadow of your dark strip through the foundation. Check to make sure it extends past all lines surrounding piece 1.

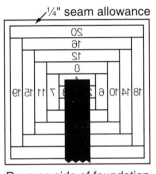

Reverse side of foundation

Diagram 2

Step 2. Position a light strip right side down on piece 1, as shown in **Diagram 3A. Note:** The dark strip added in Step 1 is under the light strip and is not visible in the diagram. Holding the fabric in position, flip the foundation to its front side, and sew on the line separating pieces 1 and 2, as shown in **3B.** Begin and end the line of stitches approximately ⅛ inch on either side of the line.

Step 3. Remove the foundation from the machine and flip it to the back side. If you used tape to secure the dark center, remove it now. Cut away the excess tail of fabric (cut just past the end of stitches, as shown in **Diagram 4A**). Flip piece 2 into a right-side-up position, finger pressing it into place. See **4B.**

Step 4. Position a light strip right side down on the

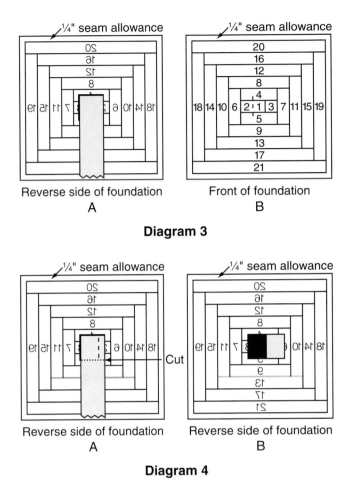

Reverse side of foundation
A

Front of foundation
B

Diagram 3

Reverse side of foundation
A

Reverse side of foundation
B

Diagram 4

opposite side of piece 1, as shown in **Diagram 5A.** Holding the strip in place, flip the foundation over and sew on the line separating piece 1 from piece 3, again beginning and ending approximately ⅛ inch on either side of the line. Remove from the machine, trim the tail, and flip piece 3 into a right-side-up position, finger pressing it into place, as shown in **5B.**

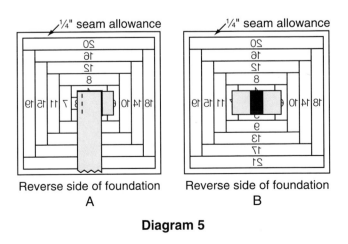

Reverse side of foundation
A

Reverse side of foundation
B

Diagram 5

Step 5. Add piece 4 in exactly the same manner. Align a dark strip right side down along the entire length of pieces 1-2-3, as shown in **Diagram 6A.** Sew, trim the tail, and finger press into place, as shown in **6B.**

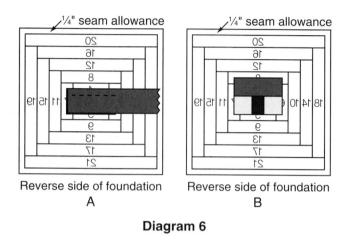

Diagram 6

Step 6. The front of your foundation should now look like **Diagram 7.** Notice that seam lines intersect each other. This crisscrossing of lines will continue, helping to stabilize your seams.

Continue to add pieces in numerical order. After the last piece (21) is sewn, press the block lightly and cut on the outermost line of the seam allowance.

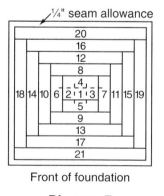

Front of foundation

Diagram 7

Step 7. Repeat, making 18 light blocks and 17 dark blocks for the crib quilt or half light blocks and half dark blocks for the double-size and queen-size quilts.

ASSEMBLING THE QUILT TOP

Step 1. Use a design wall or flat surface to arrange your blocks into a pleasing design. Use the photo on page 60, the **Double-Size Quilt Diagram,** or your own shaded drawing as a guide to block placement.

The quilt diagram illustrates the layout of the double-size quilt, which has 10 rows of 9 blocks each. The layout for the other two quilts is essentially the same: The crib quilt is made up of 7 rows with 5 blocks in each row, and the queen size has 12 rows of 10 blocks each. Alternate the light and dark blocks, turning the dark blocks 90 degrees clockwise.

Step 2. When you are satisfied with the layout, sew your blocks into rows, pressing the seams in opposite directions from row to row. If you are using removable foundations, tear away the portion surrounding the seam allowances where blocks were joined.

Step 3. Sew the rows together, carefully matching seams. Tear away all remaining portions of removable foundations.

QUILTING AND FINISHING

Step 1. Mark the quilt top for quilting, if desired. The quilt shown was quilted in the ditch along all seam lines.

Step 2. Regardless of which quilt size you've chosen to make, the backing will have to be pieced. To make the most efficient use of the backing yardage, piece the back for the crib- and queen-size quilts with the seams running horizontally across the quilt. For the double-size quilt, piece the back with the seams running vertically. **Diagram 8** illustrates the three quilt backs. Begin by trimming the selvages and dividing the yardage into equal pieces—two for both the crib and double sizes, and three for the queen size.

Step 3. For the crib quilt, divide one of the pieces in half lengthwise, and sew one narrow piece to each side of the full-width piece. Press the seams open.

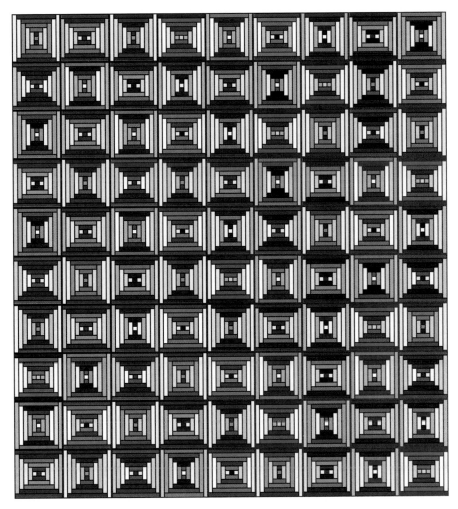

Double-Size Quilt Diagram

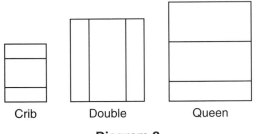

Crib   Double   Queen

Diagram 8

Step 4. For the double-size quilt, divide one of the backing pieces in half lengthwise, and sew one narrow piece to each side of the full-width piece. Press the seams open.

Step 5. For the queen-size quilt, sew two of the full-width pieces together along one long side. Divide the third piece in half lengthwise, and sew one of the halves to the joined section. Press the seams open.

Step 6. Layer the backing, batting if used, and quilt top. Baste the layers together. Quilt as desired.

Step 7. Referring to the directions on page 137 in "Quiltmaking Basics," make and attach double-fold binding. To calculate the amount of binding needed for the quilt size you are making, add up the length of the four sides of the quilt and add 9 inches. The total is the approximate number of inches of binding you will need.

Courthouse Steps
Color Plan

Photocopy this page and use it to experiment with color schemes for your quilt.

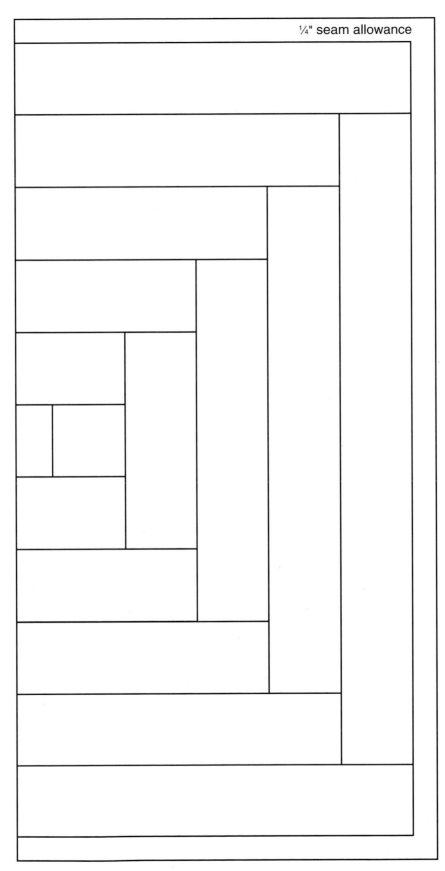

¼" seam allowance

One-Half of Block Pattern

SUMMER NIGHT

Skill Level: *Intermediate*

I nspired by the memory of a childhood friend and long summer evenings spent playing outside, Summer Night is a wonderful example of how the traditional Log Cabin block can be used to create a striking, contemporary quilt. Careful use of color and value create a starburst center and subtle shading around this wallhanging's perimeter.

BEFORE YOU BEGIN

The directions for this quilt are written based on using the foundation technique, which will make piecing the narrow (½-inch finished width) logs easier. Read through the general construction directions in "Log Cabin Basics," beginning on page 118, to become familiar with the technique. Prepare a foundation for each block using the pattern on page 74. The pattern given is reduced; enlarge it 150 percent before tracing.

While either permanent or removable foundations will work equally well for this block, permanent foundations may add enough depth to eliminate the need for batting.

CHOOSING FABRICS

The key to this quilt lies in careful color placement. While it could technically be called a two-color quilt (blue and yellow), it is actually comprised of many different fabrics in shades of gold, light and medium yellows, and medium and dark blues. The subtle variations in color and value add to the overall impact of the quilt.

There are nine different color variations of the basic block, as illustrated by **Diagram 1** on page 70. Study the photo on the opposite page and the **Quilt Diagram** on page 73 to understand how the blocks work together.

To help develop your own unique color scheme

Quilt Size	
Finished Quilt Size	74" × 74"
Finished Block Size	10½"
Number of Blocks	49

NOTE: Because specific color and value placement is critical to the overall design of this quilt, no variations in size or layout are provided.

Materials	
Fabric	**Amount**
Light yellows	2 yards
Medium yellows and golds	2 yards
Medium blues	7 yards
Dark blues	1¼ yards
Backing	4¾ yards
Batting	80" × 80"
Binding	⅝ yard
Foundation material	5¼ yards

for the quilt, make several photocopies of the **Color Plan** on page 75, and use crayons or markers to experiment with different color arrangements. Even if you choose to make a quilt exactly like the one shown, actually filling in the colors will help you gain a better understanding of the design and will make assembly easier.

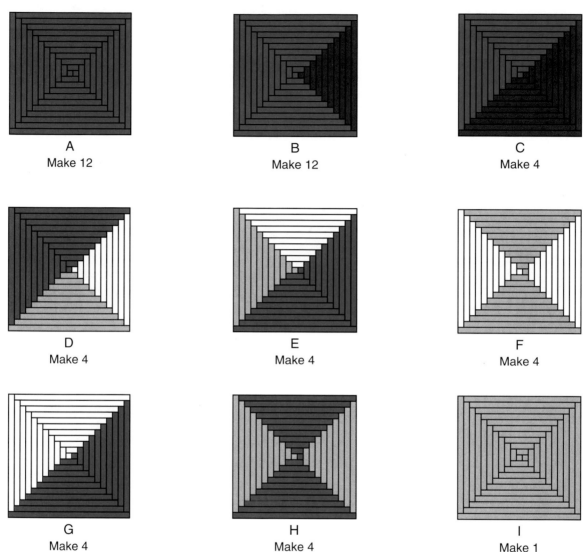

A
Make 12

B
Make 12

C
Make 4

D
Make 4

E
Make 4

F
Make 4

G
Make 4

H
Make 4

I
Make 1

Diagram 1

CUTTING

Referring to the Cutting Chart, cut the number of strips needed. Cut all strips across the fabric width (crosswise grain). **Note:** Cut and sew one sample block before cutting all the pieces for the quilt.

The pieces in the block have a finished width of ½ inch. If you were piecing traditionally, you would cut 1-inch-wide strips. For the foundation method, begin by cutting 1¼-inch strips from the fabrics. You may wish to decrease that width in ⅛-inch increments as you become more familiar with the technique, but don't cut pieces less than 1 inch wide.

The number of dark and light strips needed for logs is estimated based on using full-width yardage. If you are using scraps, the number of strips needed will vary.

Cutting Chart		
Fabric	**Strip Width**	**Number of Strips**
Light yellows	1¼"	40
Medium yellows and golds	1¼"	46
Medium blues	1¼"	180
Dark blues	1¼"	36

MAKING THE FOUNDATIONS

Step 1. The block pattern is given on page 74. Enlarge the pattern 150 percent before tracing it. **Note:** The pattern is given without seam allowances; be sure to add a ¼-inch seam allowance to all sides of the completed template.

Step 2. Following the instructions on page 123 in "Log Cabin Basics," transfer the pattern to your chosen foundation material. Make sure the marked lines are visible from the back side when you hold the foundation up to the light. Notice that the front of each foundation is a mirror image of the finished block, and always keep that in mind as you sew the logs to the foundation.

Use the **Block Diagram** as a reference for piecing order. Cut out the foundations, leaving a bit of extra material on all sides.

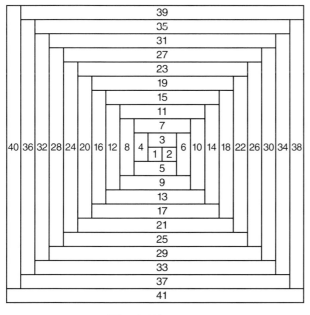

Block Diagram

PIECING THE BLOCKS

Make a sample block before cutting fabric for the entire quilt. If you experience problems while assembling the block, increase the strip width.

Using strips slightly wider than necessary can be a real time-saver since not as much precision is needed when positioning them for sewing. Reevaluate your work often. You may find that strip width can be decreased again once you are more familiar with the method.

Select one of the blocks shown in **Diagram 1** and cut several strips of the fabrics used in that block. Refer to the diagram for correct color placement as you piece your sample block.

Step 1. Cut a 1¼-inch square from the strip of fabric reserved for piece 1. Place the square right side up on the reverse side of the foundation, aligning it so that the square covers the entire area of piece 1, as shown in **Diagram 2**. Secure in place with tape, a bit of glue stick, or a pin. **Note:** Only the center portion of the block is shown in **Diagrams 2** through **6**. The complete block contains 41 logs, as shown in the **Block Diagram**.

Hold the foundation up to the light with the back side away from you. You should be able to see a shadow of the center square. Check to make sure it extends past all lines surrounding piece 1. If it doesn't, reposition the square and check it again.

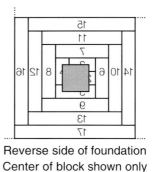

Reverse side of foundation
Center of block shown only

Diagram 2

Step 2. Place the fabric strip for piece 2 right side down on the reverse side of the foundation, as shown in **Diagram 3A** on page 72. Align the piece with the lower and left edges of piece 1. (Remember that the back of your foundation is a mirror image of the front.) Holding the fabric in position, flip the foundation to the front side and sew on the line separating pieces 1 and 2, as shown in **3B**. Begin and end the line of stitches approximately ⅛ inch on either side of the line.

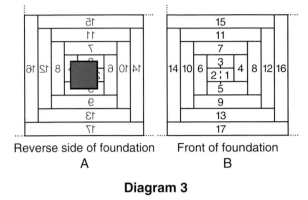

Reverse side of foundation
A

Front of foundation
B

Diagram 3

Step 3. Remove the foundation from the machine and flip it to the back side. Trim the seam allowance if necessary to reduce bulk. If you used tape to secure the center piece, remove it now. Flip piece 2 into a right-side-up position, finger pressing it into place. The reverse of your foundation should now look like **Diagram 4**. Notice that the unsewn edges of piece 2 overlap the three unsewn seam lines surrounding the piece's drawn border.

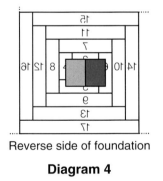

Reverse side of foundation

Diagram 4

Step 4. For piece 3, place a strip of fabric right side down, as shown in **Diagram 5A**. Holding the strip in place, flip the foundation over and sew on the line separating pieces 1 and 2 from piece 3, again beginning and ending approximately ⅛ inch on either side of the line. Remove the foundation from the machine and flip it to the back side. Cut away the excess tail of fabric, trimming just past the end of the line of stitches.

Flip piece 3 into a right-side-up position, finger pressing it into place, as shown in **5B**.

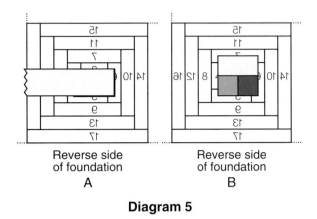

Reverse side
of foundation
A

Reverse side
of foundation
B

Diagram 5

Step 5. Piece 4 is added next. Position a strip right side down on the reverse side of your foundation. Hold the fabric in place, flip to the front of the foundation, and sew on the line separating pieces 1 and 3 from piece 4. Remove from the machine, trim the excess fabric, and flip piece 4 into a right-side-up position. Finger press firmly into place. Check to make sure all unsewn edges of piece 4 overlap seam lines around the piece's border.

The front of your foundation should now look like the one illustrated in **Diagram 6**. So far, you have sewn three seams. Notice that they cross each other. This crisscrossing will continue, helping to reinforce the seams in your foundation block.

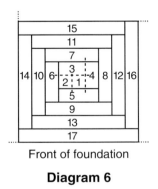

Front of foundation

Diagram 6

Step 6. Add all remaining logs in exactly the same manner. Remember to trim excess bulk from seam allowances, finger press each piece into place, and check to make sure the new piece overlaps all unsewn seam lines before adding the next log.

After you have added piece 41, press the block with a warm iron, then cut on the outer line of the seam allowance.

Step 7. Repeat Steps 1 through 6 to make the correct number of blocks in each color variation shown in **Diagram 1** on page 70. Pin a letter label to each group of blocks as you complete it.

ASSEMBLING THE QUILT TOP

Step 1. The blocks are arranged in seven rows, each containing seven blocks. Referring to **Diagram 1** on page 70, **Diagram 7**, and the **Quilt Diagram,** lay out the blocks. **Diagram 1** shows the nine block variations used; **Diagram 7** and the **Quilt Diagram** show the position of the blocks in the layout. Check to make sure the blocks are turned the right way to accurately create the design.

Step 2. Sew the blocks into rows. Tear away removable foundations from seam allowances where blocks were joined. To help you match seams perfectly, be sure to press seam allowances of adjoining rows in opposite directions.

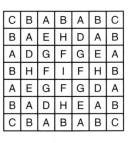

C	B	A	B	A	B	C
B	A	E	H	D	A	B
A	D	G	F	G	E	A
B	H	F	I	F	H	B
A	E	G	F	G	D	A
B	A	D	H	E	A	B
C	B	A	B	A	B	C

Diagram 7

Note: If permanent foundations create too much bulk when pressed in one direction, press the seams open. Be sure to pin and match seams carefully when rows are sewn together.

Step 3. Sew the rows together, carefully matching seams where blocks are joined.

QUILTING AND FINISHING

Step 1. Mark the quilt top for quilting, if desired. The quilt shown is quilted in the ditch along all seam lines.

Quilt Diagram

Step 2. To piece the backing, cut the 4¾-yard length of backing fabric in half crosswise, and trim the selvages. Divide one piece in half lengthwise, and sew one half to each side of the full-width piece. Press the seams open.

Step 3. Layer the backing, batting if used, and quilt top, and baste the layers together. Quilt as desired.

Step 4. Referring to the directions on page 137 in "Quiltmaking Basics," make and attach double-fold binding. You will need approximately 305 inches of binding.

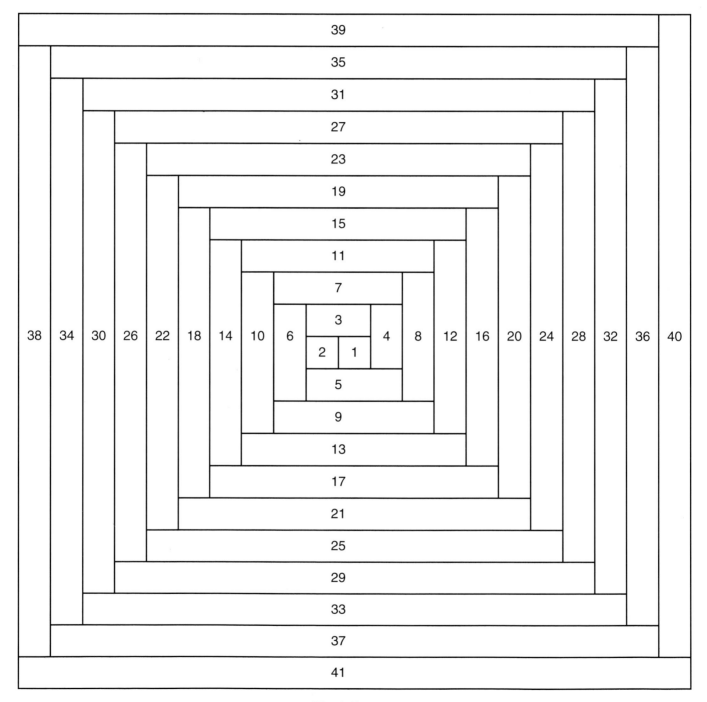

Block Pattern

Pattern shown is the mirror image of the finished block.
Note: Pattern is reduced. Enlarge it 150 percent before tracing.

Summer Night

Color Plan

Photocopy this page and use it to experiment with color schemes for your quilt.

STRAIGHT FURROWS

Skill Level: *Easy*

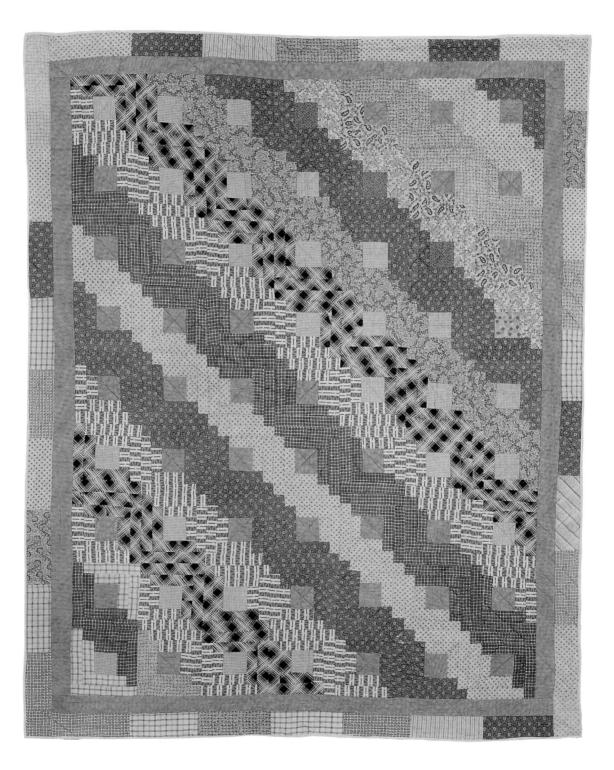

The light and dark rows of this charming 1930s lap-size quilt are reminiscent of the play of light on the furrows of a field freshly plowed and ready for planting. Warm earth tones with bright accents of blue and green add to the cozy, homespun feeling of this traditional favorite.

Before You Begin

The directions for this quilt are written based on using the chain-piecing technique, in which all the logs are cut to length and the blocks are pieced in assembly line fashion. Since the pieces are fairly large and there are only nine in each block, this is the fastest and most efficient assembly method for this quilt. Read through the general construction directions in "Log Cabin Basics," beginning on page 118, to become familiar with the technique. If you prefer to use the foundation method, prepare a foundation for each block using the pattern on page 83, and refer to page 121 in "Log Cabin Basics" for piecing instructions.

Quilt Sizes

	Lap (shown)	Double	Queen
Finished Quilt Size	63" × 78"	85½" × 100½"	93" × 100½"
Finished Block Size	7½"	7½"	7½"
Number of Blocks	63	120	132

Materials

Fabric	Lap	Double	Queen
Lights	2¼ yards	3¾ yards	4 yards
Darks	2½ yards	4½ yards	4⅞ yards
Medium	1¼ yards	1¾ yards	1¾ yards
Backing	5 yards	8¼ yards	8¾ yards
Batting	69" × 84"	92" × 107"	99" × 107"
Binding	⅝ yard	¾ yard	¾ yard

Note: Yardages are based on 44/45-inch-wide fabrics that are at least 42 inches wide after preshrinking.

Choosing Fabrics

In this quilt, as with many Log Cabin quilts, color value is more important than the actual colors used, since it's the placement of lights and darks that creates the overall design. Most of the blocks were pieced with light fabrics in log positions 2, 3, 6, and 7 and dark fabrics in log positions 4, 5, 8, and 9. In a few of the blocks, the quiltmaker reversed the light and dark placement, perhaps to add a little interest to the design. The center squares are all medium-value fabrics. For a detailed discussion of color value, see page 120 in "Log Cabin Basics."

Within the light and dark color scheme, the maker of this quilt used plaids and checks to great effect, including a bold green stripe and busy blue plaid. These fabrics create movement

Cutting Chart

Fabric	Strip Width	Number of Strips			Piece	Length
		Lap	Double	Queen		
Lights	1¾"	5	9	10	Log 2	3"
		7	14	15	Log 3	4¼"
		9	18	19	Log 6	5½"
		11	20	22	Log 7	6¾"
	3½"	4	5	6	Pieced border	9½"
Darks	1¾"	7	14	15	Log 4	4¼"
		9	18	19	Log 5	5½"
		11	20	22	Log 8	6¾"
		13	24	27	Log 9	8"
	3½"	4	6	6	Pieced border	9½"
Medium	3"	5	9	10	Center square	3"
	2¾"	7	9	9	Inner border	

and interest and help to draw the eye over the surface.

If you wish to develop your own unique color scheme, photocopy the **Color Plan** on page 82, and use crayons or colored pencils to experiment with different color arrangements.

The light and dark yardages given are generous estimates of the total yardage actually used in the quilt. Select four or five fabrics in each value to get the total yardage listed.

CUTTING

All measurements include ¼-inch seam allowances. Referring to the Cutting Chart, cut strips in the width needed, then cut the strips into logs. Cut all strips across the fabric width (crosswise grain). You may find it helpful to pin a number label to each group of logs as you cut them. **Note:** Cut and piece one sample block before cutting all the pieces for the quilt.

PIECING THE FIRST BLOCK

Refer to "Log Cabin Basics," beginning on page 118, and read through the directions for the technique you have chosen. Piece a sample block first;

it will allow you to become acquainted with the technique and to double-check the accuracy of your seam allowances. Cut enough logs for one sample block, and use the **Block Diagram** as a color sample and a guide to piecing order. The completed block should measure 7½ inches square.

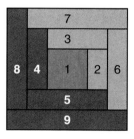

Block Diagram

Step 1. Using a ¼-inch seam allowance, sew a center piece 1 to a light log 2, as shown in **Diagram 1.** Press the seam allowance toward log 2.

Diagram 1

Step 2. Add a light log 3, as shown in **Diagram 2.** The length of log 3 should match the length of the partially sewn unit. If the lengths aren't the same, your ¼-inch seam allowance may need to be adjusted. If log 3 is shorter, your seam allowance may be less than ¼ inch. If log 3 is longer, your seam allowance may be more than ¼ inch. If your seam allowance is accurate, check to be sure you've carefully pressed the seam between pieces 1 and 2.

Diagram 2

Step 3. Continue to add logs in numerical order in a counterclockwise direction. Press seams as you work, always pressing toward the newest log.

PIECING THE REMAINING BLOCKS

Chain piecing can speed up the block assembly process. Instead of making one block from start to finish, perform one step at a time on all the blocks.

Step 1. Stack the light and dark logs near your sewing machine. Keep your sample block handy to use as a guide. Stitch a log 2 to a center piece 1 as described. Without removing the stitched pair from the sewing machine or lifting the presser foot, insert and sew a second pair. Continue sewing until all center sections are pieced. See **Diagram 3.**

Diagram 3

Step 2. Cut the stitched segments apart. Press each seam allowance toward log 2. In the same manner, add the remaining logs to the blocks until you have completed all the blocks.

ASSEMBLING THE QUILT TOP

Step 1. Using a design wall or flat surface, lay out your blocks in a pleasing arrangement. Use the

·········· Sew Quick ··········

When chain piecing, you might find it easier to work in groups of blocks rather than working on all of the quilt's blocks at one time. You'll still save lots of time using the chain-piecing method, but piecing a dozen blocks at a time from start to finish will give you a sense of accomplishment and let you see some real progress.

photo on page 76, the **Lap-Size Quilt Diagram** on page 80, or your own color drawing as a guide. The quilt diagram illustrates the layout of the lap-size quilt, which has 9 rows of 7 blocks each. The layout for the other two quilts is essentially the same: The double quilt has 12 rows of 10 blocks each and the queen-size quilt has 12 rows of 11 blocks each.

Step 2. When you are pleased with the arrangement, sew the blocks into rows, pressing the seams in opposite directions from row to row.

Step 3. Sew the rows together, carefully matching seams where blocks meet. If you've pressed the seam allowances in opposite directions, the seams should fit tightly against each other.

ADDING THE INNER BORDER

The procedure for adding borders is the same for all three quilt sizes. Prepare the strips first, then add them to the quilt according to the directions below.

Step 1. For the lap-size quilt, sew four 2¾-inch inner border strips together in pairs, making two long side borders. For the top and bottom borders, cut a fifth strip in half crosswise, and sew one half each to the two remaining border strips.

Step 2. For the double and queen-size quilts, sew eight of the 2¾-inch inner border strips together in pairs. Cut the remaining strip in half crosswise, and sew one half each to two of the long border strips.

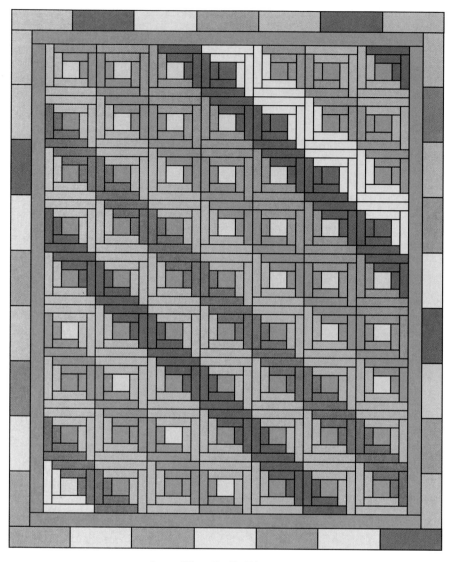

Lap-Size Quilt Diagram

Step 3. Once the border strips are prepared, measure the quilt from top to bottom, taking the measurement through the vertical center of the quilt, not at the sides. Cut the two longest strips to this length.

Step 4. Fold one strip in half crosswise and crease. Unfold it and position it right side down along one side of the quilt top, with the crease at the horizontal midpoint. Pin at the midpoint and ends first, then along the length of the entire side, easing in fullness if necessary. Sew the border to the quilt top using a ¼-inch seam allowance. Press the seam allowance toward the border. Repeat on the opposite side.

Step 5. Measure the width of the quilt, taking the measurement through the horizontal center of the quilt and including the side borders. Cut the remaining two border strips to this length.

Step 6. In the same manner as for the side borders, position and pin one strip to one end of the quilt top. Stitch and press the seam toward the border. Repeat on the opposite end.

ADDING THE PIECED BORDER

The outer border in the quilt shown is pieced with 9-inch-long segments of the same fabrics used in the blocks. Lay out and piece the four long border strips first, then add them to the quilt sides and then to the top and bottom.

Step 1. For the lap-size quilt, lay out four dark and four light segments for each side border, and four dark and three light segments for each top and bottom border.

Step 2. For the double quilt, lay out six dark and five light strips for each side border, and five dark and five light strips for each top and bottom border.

Step 3. For the queen-size quilt, lay out six dark and six light strips for each side border, and five dark and five light strips for each top and bottom border.

Step 4. When you are pleased with the arrangement, sew the strips together end to end, using accurate ¼-inch seam allowances.

Step 5. In the same manner as for the inner border, measure the length of the quilt, trim the strips to length, and stitch the side borders to the quilt. Repeat for the top and bottom pieced borders.

QUILTING AND FINISHING

Step 1. Mark the quilt top for quilting. The antique quilt shown has a 1-inch diagonal grid quilted over the whole surface.

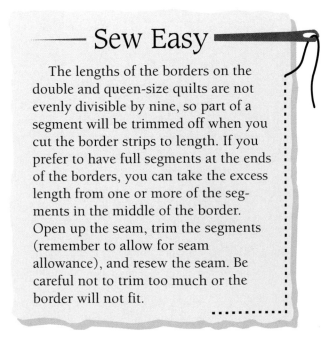

— Sew Easy ——

The lengths of the borders on the double and queen-size quilts are not evenly divisible by nine, so part of a segment will be trimmed off when you cut the border strips to length. If you prefer to have full segments at the ends of the borders, you can take the excess length from one or more of the segments in the middle of the border. Open up the seam, trim the segments (remember to allow for seam allowance), and resew the seam. Be careful not to trim too much or the border will not fit.

Step 2. Regardless of which quilt size you've chosen to make, the backing will have to be pieced. To make the most efficient use of the yardage, piece the back for the lap-size quilt with the seams running vertically across the quilt. For the double and queen-size quilts, piece the back with the seams running horizontally. **Diagram 4** illustrates the three quilt backs.

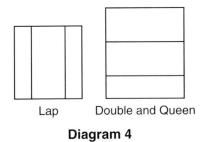

Lap   Double and Queen
Diagram 4

Step 3. For the lap quilt, divide the backing fabric crosswise into two equal pieces (each approximately 90 inches long), and trim the selvages. Divide one of the pieces in half lengthwise, and sew one half to each side of the full-width piece. Press the seams open.

Step 4. The backings for the double and the queen-size quilts are the same length, but two different widths. Begin by dividing the backing fabric into three equal pieces (approximately 99 inches each for the double and 105 inches each for the queen) and trimming the selvages. The pieced backing should measure approximately 112 inches long. Sew two of the pieces together along the long side and press the seam open. Measure the width of this piece and subtract that number from 112. The result is the amount that must be added from the third piece. Cut the piece and add it to the larger joined piece. Press the seams open.

Step 5. Layer the backing, batting, and quilt top, then baste. Quilt as desired.

Step 6. Referring to the directions on page 137 in "Quiltmaking Basics," make and attach double-fold binding. To calculate the amount of binding needed for the quilt size you are making, add up the length of the four sides of the quilt and add 9 inches. The total is the approximate number of inches of binding you will need.

Straight Furrows
Color Plan

Photocopy this page and use it to experiment with color schemes for your quilt.

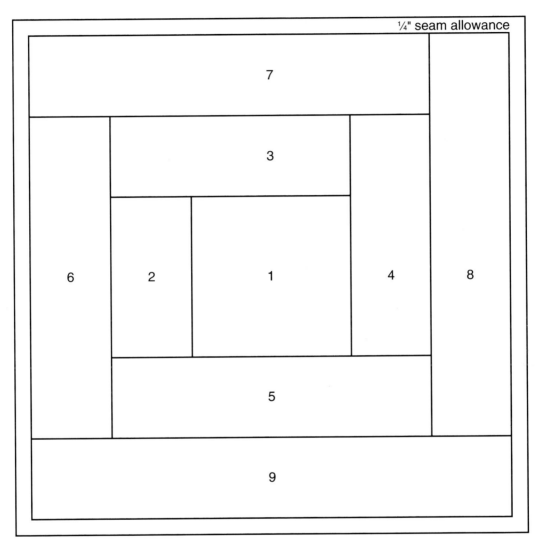

Block Pattern

Pattern shown is the mirror image of the finished block.
Note: Pattern is reduced. Enlarge it 150 percent before tracing.

PINEAPPLE VARIATION
Skill Level: *Intermediate*

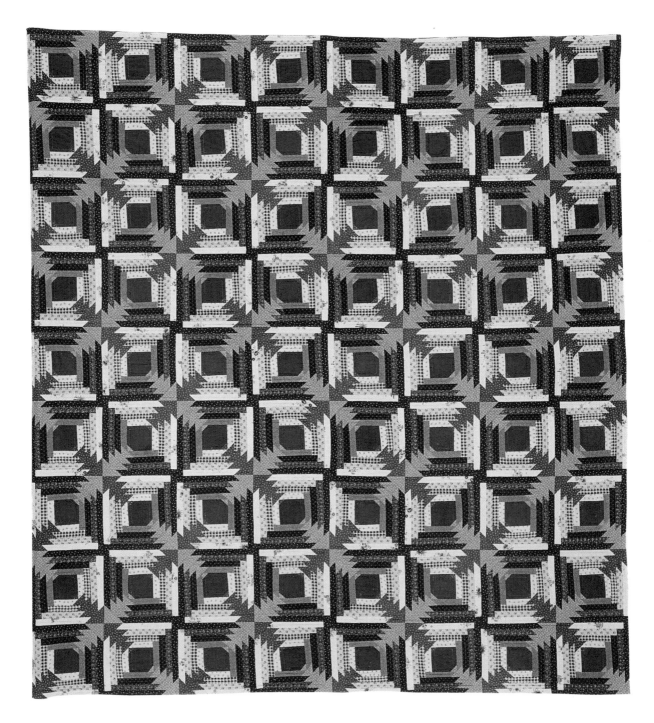

T he basic block in this queen-size quilt is an interesting combination of the traditional Log Cabin and Pineapple blocks. Alternate blocks are rotated, creating a delightful sense of movement and giving the quilt a scrappy feel.

BEFORE YOU BEGIN

The directions for this quilt are written based on using the foundation method, which makes it easier to handle the block corner triangles. Read through the general construction directions in "Log Cabin Basics," beginning on page 118, to become familiar with the foundation technique. Prepare a foundation for each block using the full-size patterns on pages 90–92. The pattern is given in three pieces. Referring to the **Pattern Key** on page 91, trace the pieces and carefully join them to complete the template.

CHOOSING FABRICS

Each block in this quilt is made from the same 11 fabrics, but the layout, with alternate blocks rotated, gives the quilt a scrappy appearance. The **Block Diagram** on page 86 shows the arrangement of color value in the block.

To develop your own unique color scheme for the quilt, make several photocopies of the **Color Plan** on page 93, and use crayons or colored pencils to experiment with different color arrangements.

Quilt Sizes			
	Twin	Double	Queen (shown)
Finished Quilt Size	72" × 84"	84" × 96"	96" × 108"
Finished Block Size	12"	12"	12"
Number of Blocks	42	56	72

Materials			
	Twin	Double	Queen
Brown	¾ yard	1 yard	1⅛ yards
Green	1½ yards	1½ yards	1⅞ yards
Gold	1½ yards	1½ yards	1⅞ yards
Light 1	⅝ yard	¾ yard	⅞ yard
Light 2	¾ yard	1 yard	1¼ yards
Light 3	⅞ yard	1⅛ yards	1½ yards
Light 4	1 yard	1⅜ yards	1¾ yards
Dark 1	⅝ yard	⅞ yard	1 yard
Dark 2	⅞ yard	1⅛ yards	1½ yards
Dark 3	1 yard	1⅜ yards	1¾ yards
Dark 4	1⅜ yards	1⅞ yards	2¼ yards
Backing	5½ yards	8¼ yards	9 yards
Batting (optional)	78" × 90"	90" × 102"	102" × 114"
Binding	¾ yard	¾ yard	⅞ yard
Foundation material	5¼ yards	7 yards	8⅞ yards

NOTE: Yardages are based on 44/45-inch-wide fabrics that are at least 42 inches wide after preshrinking.

If you want to make the quilt using dark and light scraps for the logs, simply add up the total yardage for each color value to find the approximate total you'll need. For a successful scrap quilt,

85

Cutting Chart

Fabric	Piece	Strip Width	Number of Strips		
			Twin	Double	Queen
Brown	1	4½"	5	7	8
Green	2	2¼"	2	2	2
	8	3"	2	2	3
	14	3⅝"	2	3	4
	20 & 26	4⅛"	6	6	8
Gold	3	2¼"	2	2	2
	9	3"	2	2	3
	15	3⅝"	2	3	4
	21 & 27	4⅛"	6	6	8
Light 1	4 & 5	1⅝"	10	13	16
Light 2	10 & 11	1⅝"	14	19	24
Light 3	16 & 17	1⅝"	17	23	29
Light 4	22 & 23	1⅝"	21	28	36
Dark 1	6 & 7	1⅝"	12	16	21
Dark 2	12 & 13	1⅝"	17	23	29
Dark 3	18 & 19	1⅝"	21	28	36
Dark 4	24 & 25	1⅝"	28	38	48

Sew Easy

If choosing colors seems at first to be an overwhelming task, begin by filling in the **Color Plan** with only a lead pencil, sketching areas with more or less pressure to obtain shades of gray. Color choice is often easier once you have established which areas of the block should be light, medium, and dark in value. See "Log Cabin Basics" for a detailed discussion of color value.

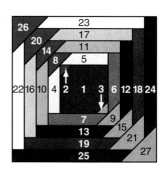

Block Diagram

CUTTING

Referring to the Cutting Chart, cut the number of strips needed. Cut all strips across the fabric width (crosswise grain). **Note:** Cut and sew one sample block before cutting all of the pieces for the quilt.

The cut sizes for the logs and triangles are slightly larger than necessary. The excess fabric makes it easier to quickly align a piece with the foundation without worrying about a shortage of seam allowance when that piece is later flipped into

variety is important, so you will likely start out with more yardage than you'll actually use. For best results, don't use scraps for the triangles; the pattern will show up best if the triangles are made from only two colors throughout.

place. After making a few blocks, you may want to alter cut sizes to suit your own sewing style.

To make the triangles for the corner pieces, cut green and gold strips in the widths indicated, cut the strips into squares, and cut each square in half diagonally.

The number of dark and light strips needed for logs is estimated based on using full-width yardage. If you are using scraps, the number of strips needed will vary.

MAKING THE FOUNDATIONS

Step 1. The pattern for the block is given full size in three parts on pages 90–92. Trace patterns A and B, then trace pattern C twice. Referring to the **Block Diagram** and to the **Pattern Key** on page 91, carefully join the four pieces to complete the block template.

Step 2. Following the instructions on page 123 in "Log Cabin Basics," transfer the pattern to the foundation material you have chosen. Make sure all of the marked lines are visible from the back side when you hold the foundation up to the light. Use the **Block Diagram** as a color sample and a reference for piecing order. Cut out the foundations, leaving a bit of extra material on all sides.

PIECING THE BLOCKS

Make a sample block before cutting fabric for the entire quilt. If you experience problems while assembling the block, increase the strip width. Reevaluate your work often. You may find that strip width can be decreased again once you are more familiar with the technique.

To ensure the correct placement of the fabrics, refer to the **Fabric Key** while piecing the blocks.

Fabric Key

■ Brown	■ Dark fabrics
▨ Gold	□ Light fabrics
■ Green	

Step 1. Cut the 4½-inch-wide strips into 4½-inch squares for the block centers. Place a square right side up on the back side of a foundation. Tack it in place with tape, a bit of glue stick, or a pin.

Hold the foundation up to the light with the back side away from you. You should be able to see a shadow of the center square through the foundation. Check to make sure it extends past all lines surrounding piece 1. If it doesn't, reposition the square and check again.

Step 2. Place a green piece 2 triangle right side down on the square, as shown in **Diagram 1A**. Holding the triangle in place, flip the foundation to the front side. Sew on the line separating piece 1 from piece 2, beginning and ending the line of stitches approximately ⅛ inch on either side of the line, as shown in **1B**.

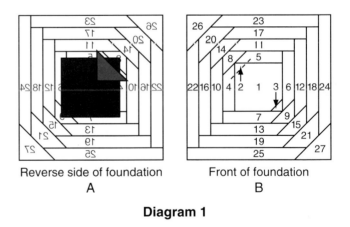

Reverse side of foundation
A

Front of foundation
B

Diagram 1

Step 3. Remove the foundation from the sewing machine and flip it to its reverse side. Trim away excess seam allowance along the seam you just stitched, then flip piece 2 into a right-side-up position and finger press firmly into place. Hold the foundation up to the light with the back side away from you. Check to make sure the shadow of piece 2 overlaps all unsewn lines around its perimeter. If you used tape to secure the center square, remove it now.

Step 4. Add the gold piece 3 triangle to piece 1 in exactly the same way. The reverse side of your foundation should now resemble **Diagram 2** on page 88.

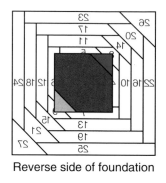

Reverse side of foundation

Diagram 2

Step 5. Piece 4 is sewn from one of the 1⅝-inch-wide strips of light fabric cut for logs. Position a strip right side down along the side of pieces 1 and 2, as shown in **Diagram 3.**

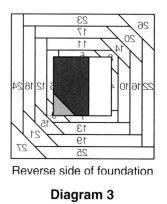

Reverse side of foundation

Diagram 3

Step 6. Holding the strip in place, flip the foundation to the front. Sew on the vertical line separating pieces 1 and 2 from piece 4, beginning and ending approximately ⅛ inch on either side of the line. Remove the foundation from the machine and flip it to the reverse side. Trim the excess tail of fabric from the strip (cut just past the end of the stitch line). Trim excess fabric from the seam allowance if necessary, then finger press piece 4 firmly into place. Hold the foundation up to the light to make sure the fabric overlaps the perimeter of piece 4.

Step 7. Sew logs 5, 6, and 7 in exactly the same manner. Log 5 is a light strip; logs 6 and 7 are dark.

Step 8. Referring to the **Block Diagram** on page 86 for correct color placement, sew triangles

for pieces 8 and 9 as you did for the previous two triangles, then add the next group of four logs (10 through 13). Continue adding pieces in numerical order until the block is finished. Be sure to trim excess seam allowances as you work and finger press the pieces firmly in place.

Step 9. Press the block, then cut on the outermost edges of the foundation. Do not tear away removable foundations at this time. Repeat the assembly steps, making the number of blocks required for your quilt.

ASSEMBLING THE QUILT TOP

Step 1. Use a design wall or flat surface to arrange your blocks into rows. Use the photo on page 84, the **Queen-Size Quilt Diagram,** or your own Color Plan as a guide to block placement. The quilt shown in the quilt diagram has nine rows of eight blocks each. The layout for the other two sizes is the same, except that the twin size has seven rows of six blocks each and the double has eight rows of seven blocks each.

Step 2. Sew the blocks together into rows, pressing the seams in opposite directions from row to row. **Note:** Permanent foundations create additional bulk in the seam allowance. If the seams are too bulky to press to one side, it may be necessary to press them open. Be sure to match and pin pressed-open seams carefully when rows are joined.

Step 3. Sew the rows together, aligning seams where blocks meet. Tear away all portions of removable foundations.

QUILTING AND FINISHING

Step 1. Mark the quilt top for quilting, if desired. The quilt shown has been quilted down the center of each log.

Step 2. Regardless of which quilt size you've chosen to make, the backing will have to be pieced. For the double and queen-size quilts, you will make the most efficient use of the yardage

Queen-Size Quilt Diagram

by piecing the back with the seams running horizontally across the quilt. For the twin-size quilt, the seams run vertically. **Diagram 4** illustrates the three quilt backs.

Step 3. For the twin-size quilt, divide the 5½-yard piece of backing fabric in half cross-

wise, and trim the selvages. Cut one of the pieces in half lengthwise, and sew one half to each side of the full-width piece. Press the seams open.

Step 4. For the double quilt, the backing should be approximately 96 × 108 inches. Cut the 8¼-yard piece of backing fabric crosswise into three equal pieces, and trim the selvages. Sew the three panels together along the long edges, and press the seams open. Trim the excess length (approximately 18 inches) after you have centered the batting and quilt top on the backing.

Step 5. For the queen-size quilt, the backing should be approximately 108 × 120 inches. Cut the 9-yard piece of backing fabric crosswise into

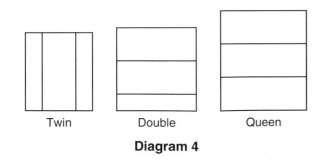

Twin   Double   Queen

Diagram 4

three equal pieces, and trim the selvages. Sew the pieces together along the long edges and press the seams open.

Step 6. Layer the quilt top, batting if used, and backing. Baste the layers together. Quilt as desired.

Step 7. Referring to the directions on page 137 in "Quiltmaking Basics," make and attach double-fold binding. To calculate the amount of binding you will need for the quilt size you are making, add up the length of the four sides of the quilt and add 9 inches. The total is the approximate number of inches of binding you will need.

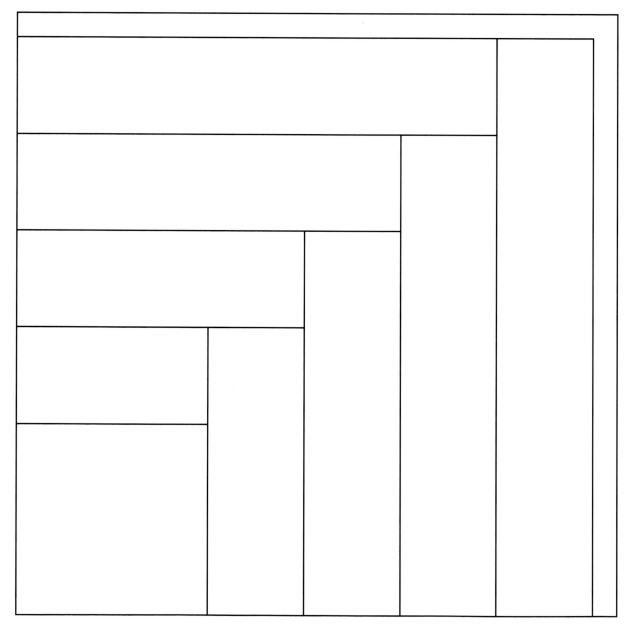

Block Pattern A

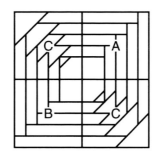

Pattern Key

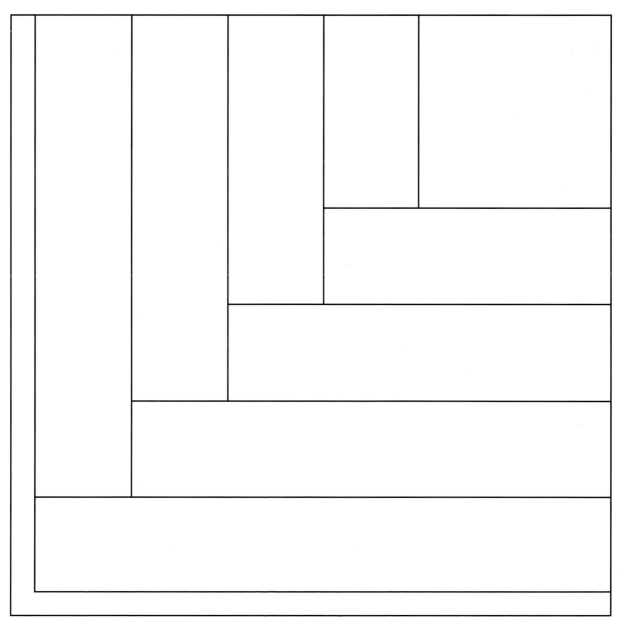

Block Pattern B

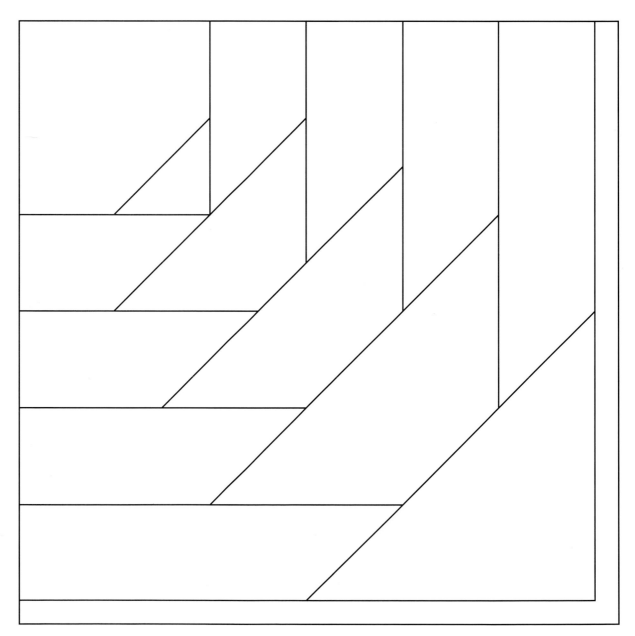

Block Pattern C

PINEAPPLE VARIATION
Color Plan

Photocopy this page and use it to experiment with color schemes for your quilt.

LOGS HEXAGONAL
Skill Level: *Challenging*

I n a unique twist on tradition, the Log Cabin blocks in this quilt are transformed into elongated hexagons. Though they look diffi-cult to construct, they are actually pieced in the same manner as a traditional block. The vibrant radiating design in this king-size quilt is achieved by combining full blocks with partial blocks.

BEFORE YOU BEGIN

Although their shape is very unusual, the blocks in this quilt, designed and made by June Ryker, are constructed in the same manner as all other Log Cabin blocks. The directions for this quilt are written based on using the foundation technique, which is an alternative to the technique June used in her original published pattern. Read through the general construction directions in "Log Cabin Basics," beginning on page 118, to become familiar with the foundation technique.

There are five different foundation templates required for this quilt, as illustrated in the **Block Diagram** on page 96. Blocks A and B are full blocks; they are made from the same template but in two different color combinations. Blocks C1 and C2 are both half blocks, and blocks D and E are partial blocks. Study **Diagram 4** on page 99 to understand how the blocks work together. Prepare a foundation for each block and partial block using the full-size patterns on pages 101–105. Both permanent and removable foundations are suitable for assembling this block.

CHOOSING FABRICS

This quilt is another example of the important role color value plays in the final layout of blocks since the positioning of darks and lights is critical for definition of the flowing design. See page 120 in "Log Cabin Basics" for a detailed description of color and value.

Quilt Size

Finished Size	99" × 99"
Number of Blocks	
Full Blocks (A&B)	48
Half Blocks (C1&C2)	8
Partial Blocks (D)	16
(E)	4

NOTE: Because the complex combination of blocks and partial blocks is critical to the overall design of this quilt, no variations in size or layout are provided.

Materials

Fabric	Amount
Light prints	7½ yards
Dark prints	8¼ yards
Solid for centers	⅝ yard
Backing	9 yards
Batting (optional)	105" × 105"
Binding	¾ yard
Foundation material	9½ yards

NOTE: Yardages are based on 44/45-inch-wide fabrics that are at least 42 inches wide after preshrinking.

To help develop your own unique color scheme for the quilt, photocopy the **Color Plan** on page 100, and use crayons or colored pencils to experiment with different color arrangements.

Light and dark yardages shown are generous estimates of the total yardage actually used in the quilt. For a successful scrap quilt, use small amounts of many fabrics.

CUTTING

Referring to the Cutting Chart, cut the number of strips needed. Cut all strips across the fabric width (crosswise grain). The cut sizes for the logs are slightly wider than the finished log size plus ¼-inch seam allowances. With the foundation method, it's easier to work with slightly wider strips. You may wish to decrease the width in ⅛-inch increments as you become more familiar with the technique.

To make the block centers, first make a template of piece 1 using the pattern on page 101, and add ¼-inch seam allowances to all sides. Use the template to cut a piece 1 for each block from the 4½-inch-wide strips. **Note:** Cut and sew one sample block before cutting all the pieces for the quilt.

Cutting Chart

Fabric	Strip Width	Number of Strips
Light prints	1¾"	154
Dark prints	1¾"	168
Solid	4½"	4

The number of dark and light strips needed for logs is estimated based on using full-width yardage. If you are using scraps, the number of strips needed will vary.

MAKING THE FOUNDATIONS

Step 1. The pattern is given full size in seven pieces on pages 101–105. Make a template for each different type of block, as shown in the **Block Diagram**. For best results, first trace all of the

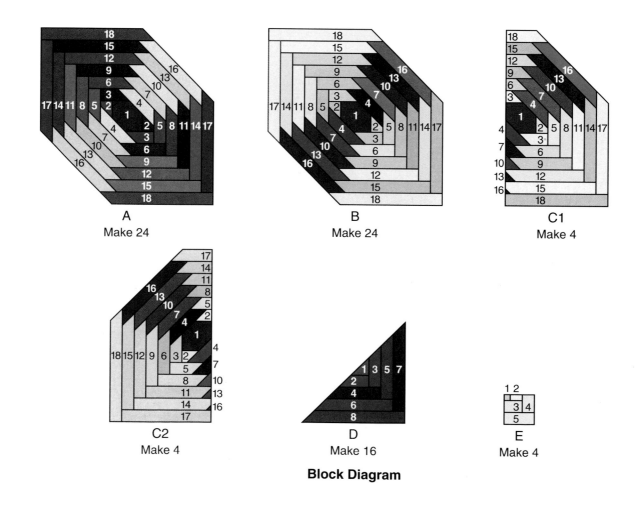

A
Make 24

B
Make 24

C1
Make 4

C2
Make 4

D
Make 16

E
Make 4

Block Diagram

pieces and carefully join them to make the template for the full block, referring to the **Pattern Key** on page 103 for correct placement. The full-block template should measure 12 inches across and 20½ inches from tip to tip. Trace the templates for the half and partial blocks from the completed full-block template. The colored lines on the pattern pieces indicate the various partial templates. Add ¼-inch seam allowances to all sides of each template.

Step 2. Following the instructions on page 123 in "Log Cabin Basics," transfer the patterns to your chosen foundation material. Make sure the marked lines are visible from the back side when you hold the foundation up to the light. Use the **Block Diagram** as a color sample and a reference for piecing order. Cut out the foundations, leaving a bit of extra material on all sides.

PIECING THE BLOCKS

Make a sample A or B block before cutting fabric for the entire quilt. If you experience problems while assembling the block, it may help to increase the width of the fabric strips slightly. Reevaluate your work often. You may find that strip width can be decreased once you are more familiar with the method.

Step 1. Cut a few 1¾-inch-wide strips of each fabric you plan to use in your sample block. Arrange the strips in piles, placing like values together. For a scrappy look, don't be concerned

Premarking your foundation for log color or value can be helpful. For this quilt, an L or a D, written with a permanent marker on specific logs to designate light or dark, would be a quick reference for piecing. Use the **Block Diagram** as a guide to value placement.

with color; just pick up the next strip of the correct value and sew.

Step 2. Place a 2½ × 4½-inch center rectangle right side up on the back of the foundation, covering the entire area of piece 1, as shown in **Diagram 1**. Secure it in place with tape, a bit of glue stick, or a pin.

Hold the foundation up to the light with the back side away from you. A shadow of the rectangle should be visible and overlap all lines surrounding piece 1. If it doesn't, reposition the fabric and check again.

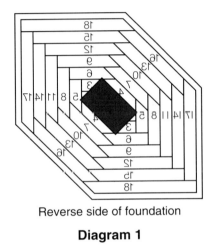

Reverse side of foundation

Diagram 1

Step 3. Add Row 2, beginning with either piece in the row. Place a strip of fabric right side down on top of piece 1, as shown in **Diagram 2A** on page 98. Holding the strip in place, flip the foundation over. Sew along the line separating piece 1 from the piece you are sewing in Row 2, beginning and ending approximately ⅛ inch on either side of the line.

Step 4. Remove the foundation from the machine and flip it to the reverse side. Trim away the excess tail of fabric just past the end of the seam line. Trim the bulk from the seam allowance, then flip the newly sewn piece into a right-side-up position. Finger press firmly in place. If you used tape on piece 1, remove it now. The reverse side of your foundation should now resemble **2B** on page 98. Notice that the unsewn edges of the new log overlap the three unsewn seam lines surrounding the piece's drawn border. Repeat to add the remaining log in Row 2.

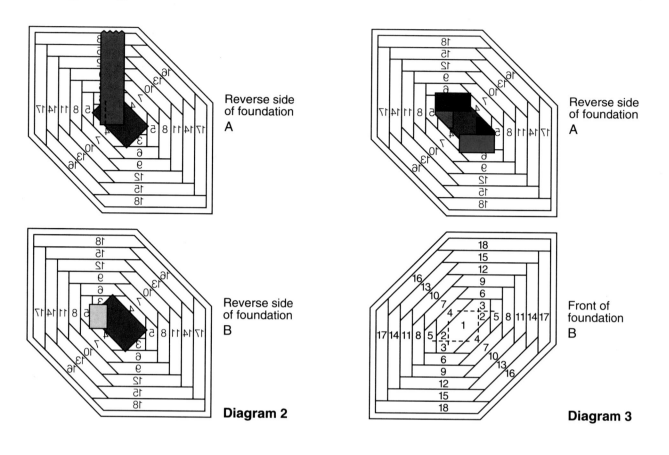

Reverse side
of foundation
A

Reverse side
of foundation
A

Reverse side
of foundation
B

Front of
foundation
B

Diagram 2

Diagram 3

Step 5. Add the two logs in Row 3 in exactly the same manner. Stitch, trim, finger press, and check the width of each new log to make sure it extends past the unsewn seam lines. The reverse side of your foundation will now resemble **Diagram 3A**, and the front of your foundation should now resemble **3B**, with sewn seam lines crisscrossing each other. These crisscrossing seam lines help to reinforce the seams and add stability.

Step 6. All remaining logs are added in the same way. Although the block may look different from other foundation-based blocks, there is actually no difference in the way logs are added. Keep working your way outward until the last logs in Row 18 are sewn. Press the completed block lightly, then cut on the outer line of seam allowance, removing excess fabric.

Step 7. Repeat Steps 2 through 6, making the required number of full, half, and partial blocks. The piecing process for the half and partial blocks is the same as for the full blocks. Always begin

with the lowest-numbered piece and work your way to the outside.

ASSEMBLING THE QUILT TOP

Step 1. Use a design wall or flat surface to arrange your blocks, referring to **Diagram 4** and the **Quilt Diagram** as guides to block placement.

Step 2. You will begin assembling the quilt at its center, radiating outward as you work. Join the blocks in the order listed below. Sew only to the outside seam line of the foundation; leave the seam allowances free. Backstitch at the beginning and the end of the seam. Pivot blocks to set in seams where necessary. (For details on setting in seams, see page 133 in "Quiltmaking Basics.")

❖ Sew four A blocks together at the quilt's center.
❖ Sew a B block into each corner.
❖ Sew two A blocks to each side.
❖ Sew two B blocks to each corner.
❖ Sew three A blocks to each side.

Quilt Diagram

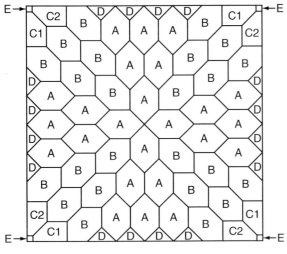

Diagram 4

✧ Sew three B blocks to each corner.

✧ Sew partial blocks C1, C2, D, and E around the outside edge to complete the quilt top.

Step 3. Tear away all removable foundations. Press seams.

QUILTING AND FINISHING

Step 1. Mark the quilt top for quilting, if desired. The quilt shown was quilted down the center of each log.

Step 2. The backing for this quilt should measure approximately 108 inches square. Cut the 9-yard piece of backing fabric into three equal lengths, and trim the selvages. Sew the segments together lengthwise. Press the seams open.

Step 3. Layer the backing, batting if used, and quilt top, centering the batting and quilt top on the backing. Trim approximately 9 inches of excess backing fabric from each side of the quilt. Baste the layers together. Quilt as desired.

Step 4. Referring to the directions on page 137 in "Quiltmaking Basics," make and attach double-fold binding. You will need approximately 405 inches of binding.

LOGS HEXAGONAL
Color Plan

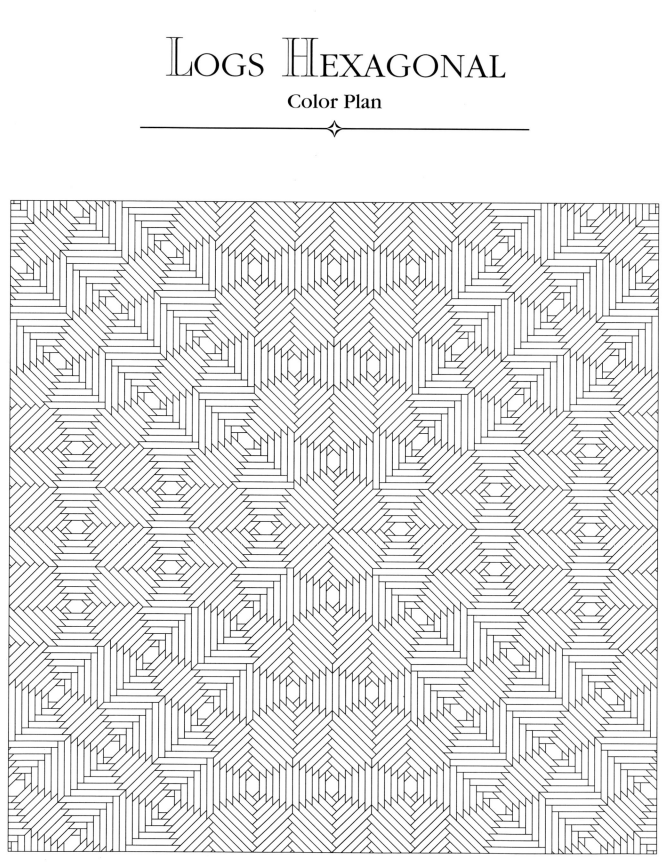

Photocopy this page and use it to experiment with color schemes for your quilt.

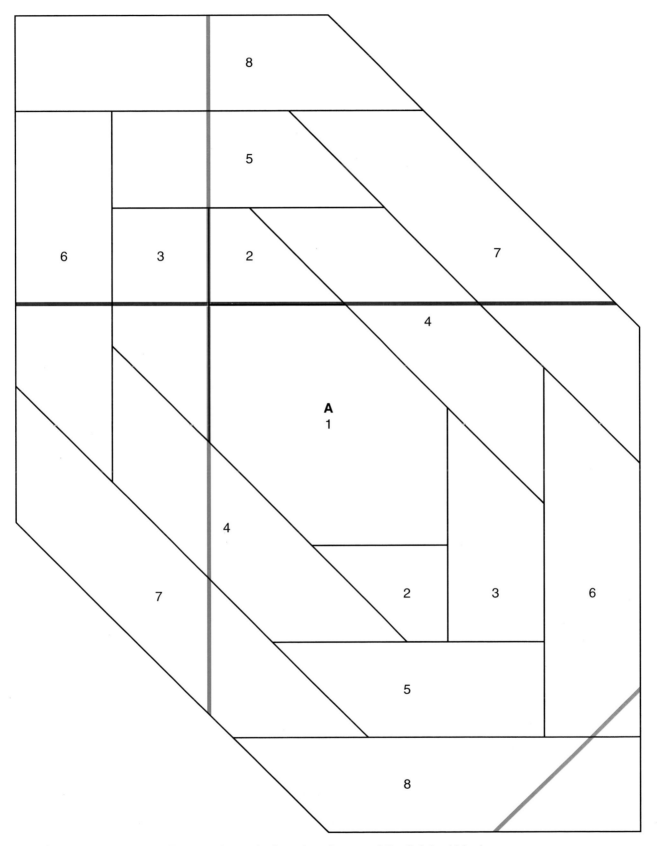

Pattern shown is the mirror image of the finished block.

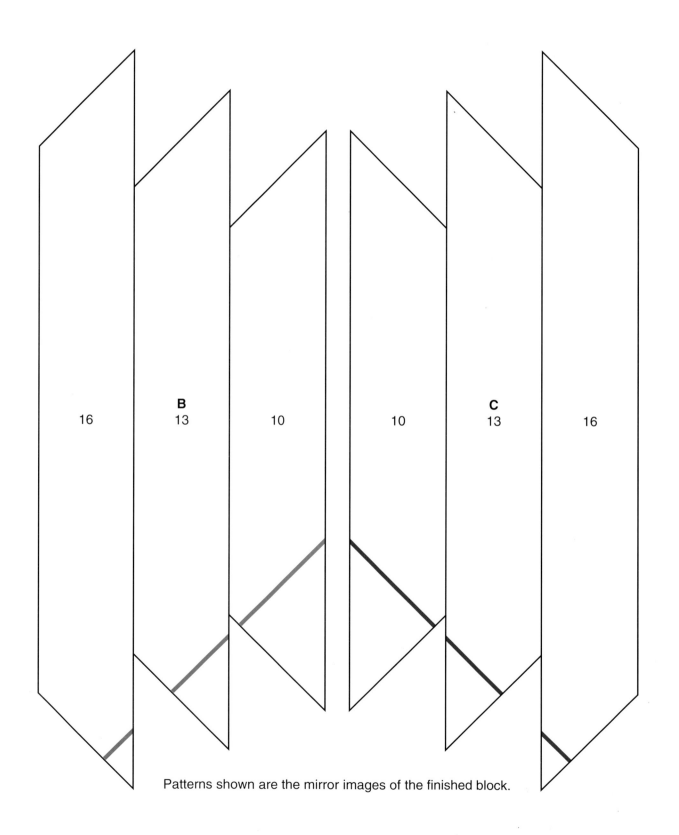

Patterns shown are the mirror images of the finished block.

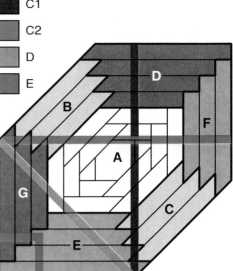

Pattern Key

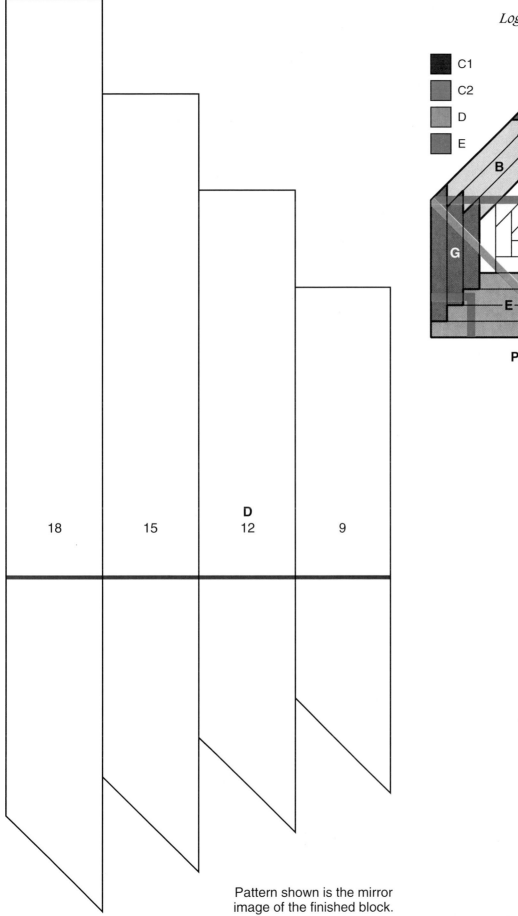

18   15   **D** 12   9

Pattern shown is the mirror
image of the finished block.

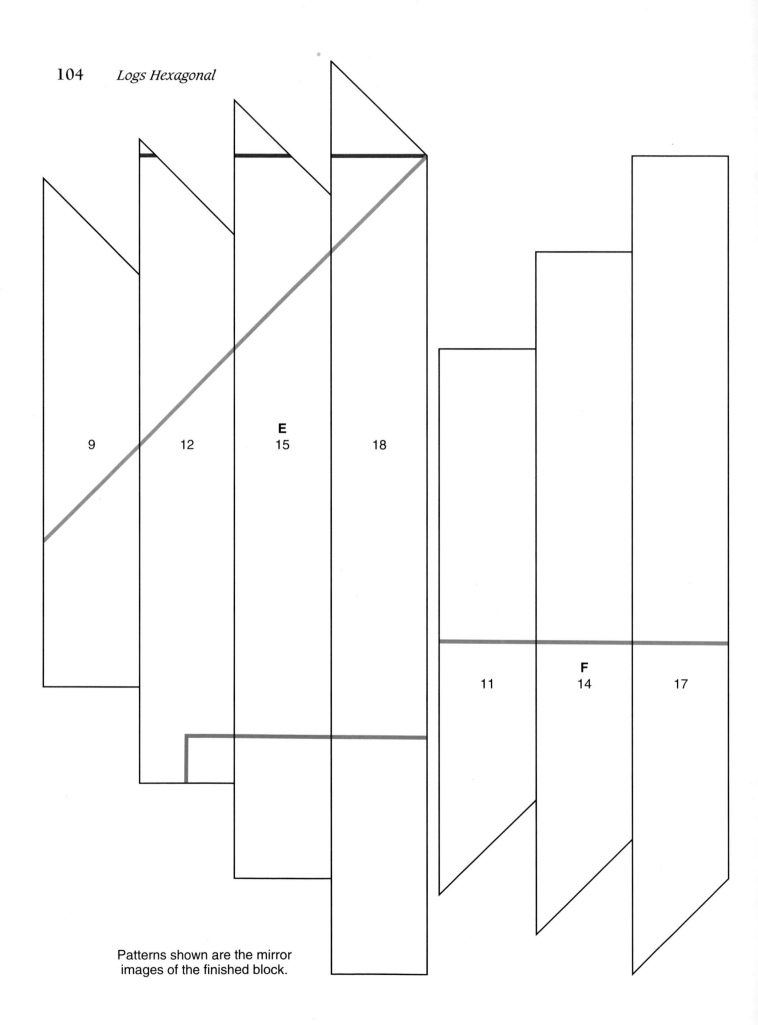

9

12

E
15

18

11

F
14

17

Patterns shown are the mirror
images of the finished block.

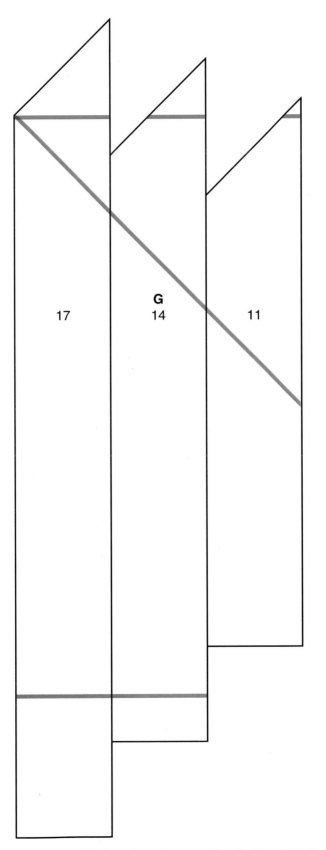

17   **G** 11
      14

Pattern shown is the mirror image of the finished block.

This striking queen-size quilt is thought to have been made by Lillie A. Miller Rohrbach, a Mennonite woman born in 1876 in Upper Hanover Township, Pennsylvania. The limited color palette coupled with an unusual setting creates a graphic image not often seen in a Log Cabin quilt. The curves of the cable quilting design in the triple borders provide an interesting counterpoint to the otherwise angular design.

Before You Begin

The directions for this quilt are written based on using the foundation technique, which will make piecing the half blocks easier. Read through the general construction directions in "Log Cabin Basics," beginning on page 118, to become familiar with the technique. Prepare a foundation for each block using one of the patterns on pages 115–117. If you are making the queen-size quilt, use the 6-inch pattern. If you are making the crib-size quilt, use the 3-inch pattern.

Quilt Sizes

	Crib	Queen (shown)
Finished Quilt Size	44" × 44"	86" × 86"
Finished Block Size	3"	6"
Number of Full Blocks		
Blue/White/Yellow	72	72
Red/White/Yellow	40	40
Number of Half Blocks		
White/Yellow	32	32

Materials

	Crib	Queen
White	2 yards	4½ yards
Blue	1¼ yards	2¾ yards
Red	⅞ yard	2⅛ yards
Yellow	⅜ yard	¾ yard
Backing	3¼ yards	8¼ yards
Batting (optional)	56" × 56"	94" × 94"
Binding	½ yard	¾ yard
Foundation material	1¾ yards	2¾ yards

NOTE: Yardages are based on 44/45-inch-wide fabrics that are at least 42 inches wide after preshrinking.

Choosing Fabrics

The simple red, blue, and yellow solids that are used in this quilt result in a very graphic image. You can substitute other solids or even prints for the colors used here and have an equally striking quilt. For best results, use colors with high contrast.

To help develop your own unique color scheme for the quilt, photocopy the **Color Plan** on page 114, and use crayons or colored pencils to experiment with different color arrangements.

Cutting Chart

Fabric	Piece	Crib		Queen	
		Strip Width	Number of Strips	Strip Width	Number of Strips
White	Border	1½"	4	3½"	8
	Logs	1"	45	1½"	77
Blue	Border	3½"	5	3½"	8
	Logs	1"	27	1½"	47
Red	Border	1½"	4	3½"	8
	Logs	1"	15	1½"	26
Yellow	Centers	1¼"	4	2"	6
		2"	1	2¾"	2

CUTTING

All measurements include seam allowances. With the foundation method, strips for logs are cut a bit wider than necessary. Referring to the Cutting Chart, cut the strips and borders needed for the quilt size you are making. Cut all strips across the fabric width (crosswise grain). **Note:** Cut and piece one sample block before cutting all the pieces for the quilt.

MAKING THE FOUNDATIONS

There are two blocks used in this quilt. One is a full block, the other a half block, as illustrated in the **Block Diagram**. The patterns for both blocks are given full size on pages 115–117.

Step 1. Trace the patterns to make templates for the size quilt you have chosen.

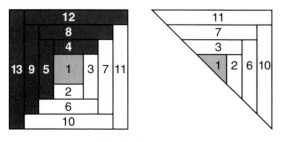

Block Diagram

Sew Easy

A mock-up foundation makes a handy piecing guide. Use markers to color in specific areas on the front, or develop a color code and transfer it to each foundation as you did with other markings. Keep the mock-up near your sewing machine and refer to it as needed.

Step 2. Following the instructions on page 123 in "Log Cabin Basics," transfer the patterns to the foundation material you have chosen. Make sure all of the lines are visible from the back side of the foundation when you hold it up to the light. Use the **Block Diagram** as a color sample and a reference for piecing order.

Step 3. Cut out the foundations, leaving a bit of excess material on all sides.

PIECING THE BLOCKS

Make a sample block before cutting fabric for the entire quilt. If you experience problems while assembling the block, increase the strip width.

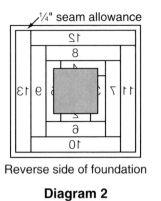

Reverse side of foundation

Diagram 2

Sew Quick

Using wider than necessary strips can be a time-saver since not as much precision is necessary when positioning strips. If you position and sew a strip with an overly large seam allowance, the extra width means chances are good that the piece will still be wide enough to compensate for an error—so no ripping out seams!

Reevaluate your work often. You may find that strip width can be decreased again once you are more familiar with the technique.

Although they look very different, the full block and the half block are pieced in exactly the same manner.

Step 1. Cut the centers of the blocks from the yellow strips. For the queen-size quilt, cut the 2-inch-wide strips into 2-inch squares for the full blocks. For the half blocks, cut the 2¾-inch strips into 2¾-inch squares, then cut the squares in half diagonally, as shown in **Diagram 1.**

For the crib quilt, cut the 1¼-inch strips into 1¼-inch squares for the full blocks. For the half blocks, cut the 2-inch strip into 2-inch squares, then cut the squares in half diagonally, as shown.

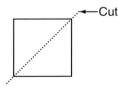

Diagram 1

Step 2. To make a full block, begin by placing a yellow square (piece 1) right side up on the back side of a full block foundation, entirely covering the area of piece 1. Secure with a strip of tape, a bit of glue stick, or a pin. See **Diagram 2.**

Step 3. Hold the foundation up to the light with the back side away from you. A shadow of the square should be visible and extend past all lines surrounding piece 1. If it doesn't, reposition the square and check again.

Step 4. Place a white strip right side down on the yellow piece 1, as shown in **Diagram 3A.** The strip should be aligned with the lower and left edges of piece 1. Holding the fabric in position, flip the foundation to its front side and sew on the line separating pieces 1 and 2, as shown in **3B.** Begin and end the line of stitches approximately ⅛ inch on either side of the line.

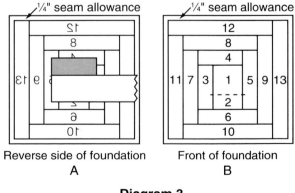

Reverse side of foundation
A

Front of foundation
B

Diagram 3

Step 5. Remove the foundation from the machine and flip it to its reverse side. Trim the excess "tail" of white fabric just to the right of your line of stitches, as shown in **Diagram 4A** on page 110. Trim the seam allowance if necessary to reduce bulk. If you used tape to secure the yellow square, remove it now. Flip piece 2 into a right-side-up position, finger pressing it into place. See **4B**. The unsewn edges of piece 2 overlap the three unsewn seam lines surrounding the piece's border.

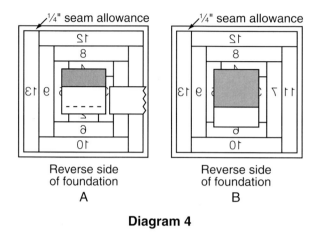

Diagram 4

Step 6. For piece 3, place a white strip right side down, as shown in **Diagram 5A**. Holding the strip in place, turn the foundation over and sew on the vertical line separating pieces 1 and 2 from piece 3, again beginning and ending approximately ⅛ inch on either side of the line. Remove from the machine, trim the tail, and flip piece 3 into a right-side-up position, finger pressing it into place, as shown in **5B**. Check to make sure all unsewn edges of piece 3 overlap the seam lines around the piece's border.

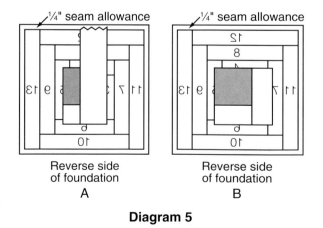

Diagram 5

Step 7. Piece 4 is either blue or red. Add it in exactly the same manner as for piece 3. When you

have added piece 4, look at the front of your foundation. So far, you have sewn three seams, as illustrated in **Diagram 6**. Notice that the seam lines intersect each other. This crisscrossing will continue, helping to stabilize the seams in your foundation block.

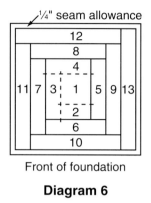

Diagram 6

Step 8. Continue to add pieces in numerical order. Remember to trim excess bulk from seam allowances, finger press each piece into place, and check to make sure that the new piece overlaps all unsewn seam lines before stitching the next strip. After you have added piece 13, press the block with a warm iron, then cut on the outer line of the seam allowances.

Step 9. Repeat Steps 2 through 8, making a total of 112 full blocks. You will need 72 blocks with blue logs and 40 blocks with red logs.

Step 10. Although the half-block template may look a bit different, the pieces are sewn in exactly the same manner as for the full blocks. Begin with the yellow center and add white pieces in numerical order.

When you position and trim strips, make sure the fabric extends past the outer perimeter of the seam allowances. Make a total of 32 half blocks.

ASSEMBLING THE QUILT TOP

Step 1. Use a design wall or flat surface to arrange your blocks. Lay out the blocks in diagonal rows, as shown in **Diagram 7**.

Diagram 7

Step 2. Sew the blocks into rows. If you used removable foundation material, tear it away from seam allowances where blocks were joined.

Step 3. Sew the rows together. To help you match seams perfectly, be sure to press seam allowances of adjoining rows in opposite directions. **Note:** If permanent foundations create too much bulk when pressed in one direction, press the seams open. Be sure to pin and match seams carefully when rows are sewn together.

Step 4. Each corner is made from two half blocks. Sew four pairs of half blocks together, as shown in **Diagram 8.** Sew a pair to each corner of your quilt top.

ADDING THE BORDERS

The procedure for adding borders is the same whether you are making the crib quilt or the

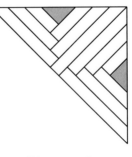

Diagram 8

queen-size quilt. However, for the queen-size quilt, you must first sew the border strips together in pairs, then trim them to the correct length. For the blue border on both quilts, it may be necessary to add parts of additional strips to each border to achieve the necessary length.

Step 1. Measure the quilt from top to bottom, taking the measurement through the vertical center of the quilt, not at the sides. Cut two red border strips to this length.

Step 2. Fold one strip in half crosswise and crease. Unfold it and position it right side down along one side of the quilt top, with the crease at the horizontal midpoint. Pin at the midpoint and ends first, then along the length of the entire side, easing in fullness if necessary. Sew the border to the quilt top using a ¼-inch seam allowance. Press the seam allowance toward the border. Repeat on the opposite side.

Step 3. Measure the width of the quilt, taking the measurement through the horizontal center of the quilt and including the side borders. Cut the remaining two red border strips to this length.

Step 4. In the same manner as for the side borders, position and pin a strip along one end of the quilt top, easing in fullness if necessary. Stitch, using a ¼-inch seam allowance. Press the seam toward the border. Repeat on the opposite end.

Step 5. In the same manner, add the white border strips to the four sides of the quilt top.

Step 6. Add the blue border strips last, using the same methods.

Step 7. Tear away all removable foundations. The completed quilt top should look like the one shown in the quilt diagrams.

QUILTING AND FINISHING

Step 1. Mark the quilt top for quilting. The antique quilt shown was quilted in the ditch on all of the blocks. A wide cable design was added in the borders.

Step 2. Regardless of which quilt size you've chosen to make, the backing will have to be pieced. For the queen-size quilt, the backing should measure approximately 94 inches square. Divide the 8¼-yard length of backing fabric crosswise into three equal 2¾-yard pieces, and trim the selvages.

Step 3. Measure the width of one of the pieces (it should be approximately 41 inches wide), and

Queen-Size Quilt Diagram

Crib-Size Quilt Diagram

subtract that number from 94 inches. This is the additional width you must add to the segment to make the backing large enough. Divide the additional width needed by two, add ¼ inch for the seam allowance, then cut a strip this width from each of the two remaining pieces.

Step 4. Sew one strip to each side of the full-width piece, as shown in **Diagram 9.** Press the seams open. Layer the backing, batting if used, and quilt top. Baste the layers together.

Step 5. For the crib quilt, divide the 3¼-yard length of fabric crosswise into two equal 1⅝-yard pieces, and trim the selvages.

Step 6. Divide one of the pieces in half lengthwise, as shown in **Diagram 9,** and sew one half to each side of the full-width piece. Press the seams open. Layer the backing, batting if used, and quilt top. Baste the layers together.

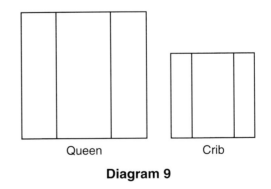

Queen   Crib

Diagram 9

Step 7. Quilt as desired.

Step 8. Referring to the directions on page 137 in "Quiltmaking Basics," make and attach double-fold binding. To calculate the amount of binding needed for the quilt size you are making, add up the length of the four sides of the quilt and add 9 inches. The total is the approximate number of inches of binding you will need.

Red, White, and Blue
Color Plan

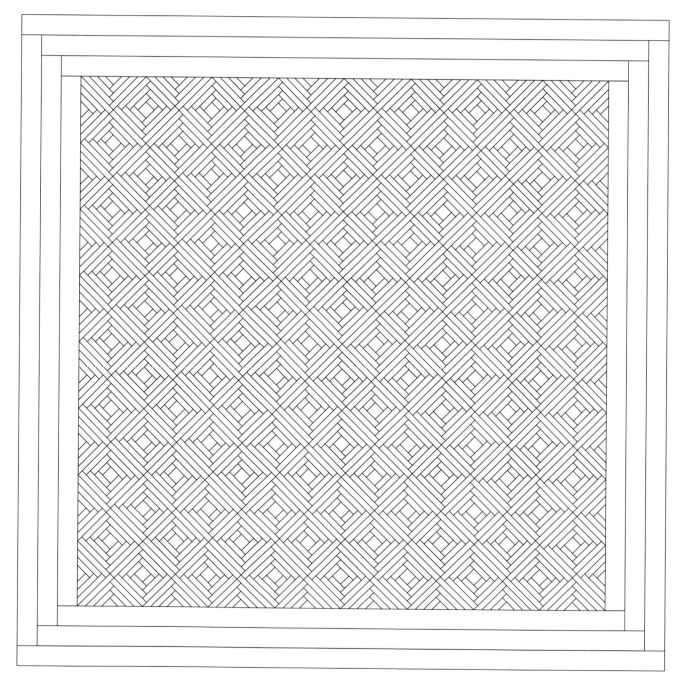

Photocopy this page and use it to experiment with color schemes for your quilt.

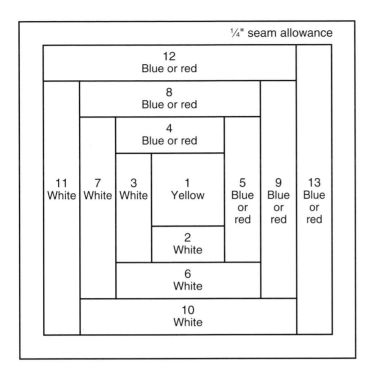

Full-Block Pattern for Crib-Size Quilt

Pattern shown is the mirror image of the finished block.

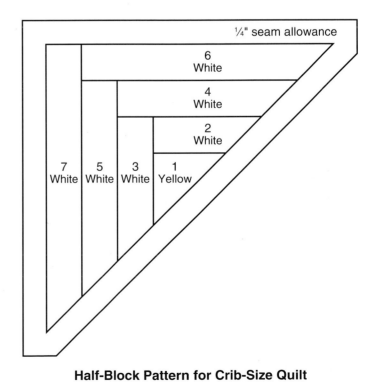

Half-Block Pattern for Crib-Size Quilt

Pattern shown is the mirror image of the finished block.

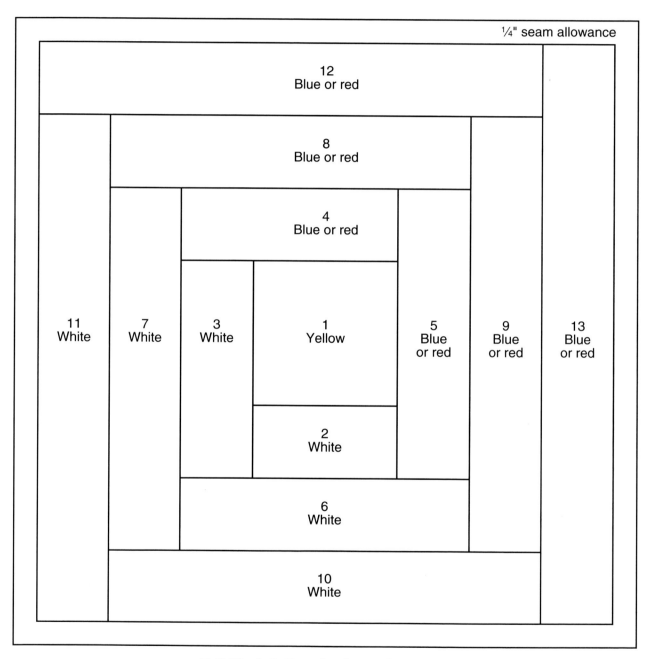

Full-Block Pattern for Queen-Size Quilt

Pattern shown is the mirror image of the finished block.

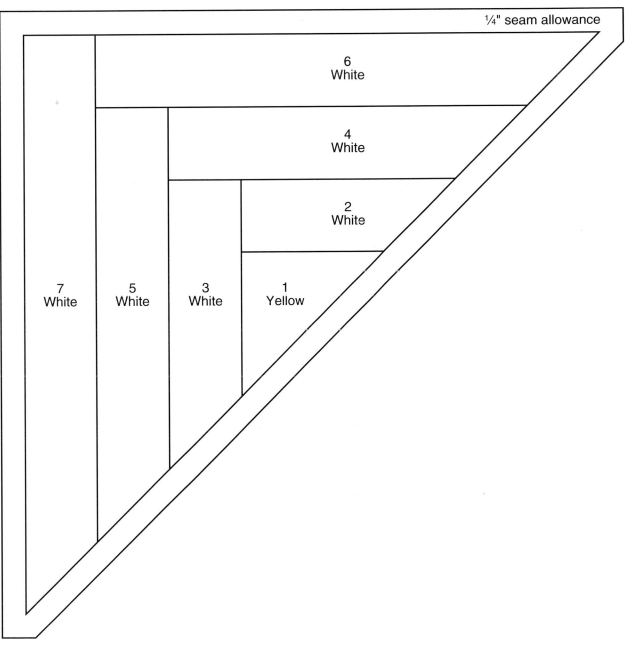

¼" seam allowance

6
White

4
White

2
White

7
White

5
White

3
White

1
Yellow

Half-Block Pattern for Queen-Size Quilt

Pattern shown is the mirror image of the finished block.

Log Cabin
Basics

The step-by-step directions for the projects in this book are based on two construction techniques: foundation piecing and chain piecing. In this section, you'll find details on each of the two techniques, as well as helpful information pertaining to Log Cabin quilts in general. It's a good idea to read through this section before beginning any of the projects in this book.

FABRIC ARRANGEMENTS

You will see Log Cabin quilts of many different kinds on the pages of this book. Some are antique, some are new quilts made in the tradition of early designs, and others are very contemporary. The potential number of designs that can be made using Log Cabin variations is limited only by your imagination.

Many Log Cabin quilts are pieced using fabric in what appears at first to be a very haphazard arrangement. When you look at a single block from a scrap quilt, it often doesn't have much impact, but when sewn together into one of the traditional settings—or a setting of your own design—the effect can be truly striking.

Whether or not you choose to work with scraps, the settings for most Log Cabin quilts more often depend on value—that is, the lightness or darkness of fabrics—than on the particular color of fabrics. **Diagram 1** illustrates a few of the traditional settings used in Log Cabin quilts. Notice how the character of the designs changes when the values are reversed or slightly altered. To experiment with different value combinations, make several photocopies of the Color Plan provided with the project you've chosen. Use color markers, or simply fill in the logs with different shades of lead pencil, to find the right combination of values for your own project.

Keep in mind that the perceived value of a fabric depends on the fabric it is positioned against. For example, medium blue looks dark when positioned against a pastel, but it looks light to medium when positioned against black.

Begin sorting fabrics by choosing a group you

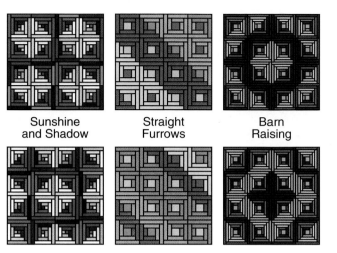

Sunshine and Shadow   Straight Furrows   Barn Raising

Diagram 1

feel are of the same value. For a true scrap quilt, pay no attention to color. Place the fabrics side by side where each will be visible in relation to the others (pinning them to a wall covered with a piece of flannel or batting works well). View the entire grouping through your value filter. The fabrics should all blend together. If any fabric appears noticeably lighter or darker than others in the group, remove it. In the example shown in

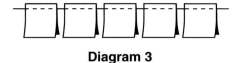
Diagram 3

Diagram 2, the second fabric from the left is noticeably darker than the others. Add and subtract fabrics until you have a good assortment for that particular value. Repeat the process for remaining value groups.

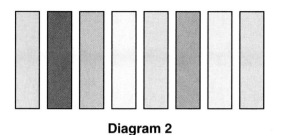
Diagram 2

If you don't have a value filter, you can sort fabrics by value by viewing them from a distance. Pin fabrics you think are the same value to a wall, then take a step back. Do the pieces blend together? Are there a few that don't seem to fit in with the others? Squinting at the fabrics may help. Again, add and subtract fabrics until you have a grouping that works.

CHOOSING A TECHNIQUE

Two different construction techniques are used to make the projects in this book: foundation piecing and chain piecing. Both techniques are described here. Each method has merit, and either can be used successfully to construct any Log Cabin block. Read through this section to determine which method best suits the project and your personal sewing style.

Chain Piecing

Some of the quilts in this book were assembled using a technique called chain piecing, or assembly line piecing, in which like segments are fed through the sewing machine one after another, without lifting the presser foot or clipping threads on individual segments. The end result is a chain of sewn segments connected to one another by a short length of thread, as shown in **Diagram 3.**

Chain piecing is a good choice if logs have a finished width of 1 inch or more. Wider strips are easier to handle than very narrow ones, and if slight variations do occur, they won't be as noticeable in a wider strip. Another benefit of chain piecing is its speed. Since it is assembly line sewing, chain piecing usually makes block construction faster. You can perform the same step on all the blocks before moving on to the next step.

One disadvantage of chain piecing is that all the logs must be cut to the exact size before sewing. There is a much greater need for precise cutting than with the foundation method, but once all the pieces are cut, the sewing is a breeze.

Foundation Piecing

Many Log Cabin designs are perfect candidates for the foundation method of piecing. Nineteenth-century quilters used this technique to construct their quilts, sewing fabric pieces to either the front or back side of a foundation onto which a copy of the block had been drafted. Foundation piecing is enjoying a strong revival today, with more and more quilters designing blocks specifically for use with this method.

Foundations help ensure that your quilt will be square. Log Cabin and Pineapple blocks won't pucker up in the middle when they are pieced on a foundation. In addition, foundation piecing is often the best choice for blocks with narrow logs. It's much easier to construct a perfect block full of ½-inch logs when those logs are sewn to a rigid foundation with premarked lines. Sewing individual narrow strips together with an exact ¼-inch seam allowance is possible, of course, but accurate results are more difficult to achieve.

One disadvantage of the foundation method is the fact that a separate foundation must be prepared for each individual block. This requires additional preparation time as well as added materials. But there are benefits that help offset this extra preparation: You save cutting time by not having to cut individual logs to exact sizes. Working with long strips that are trimmed as you go means the actual sewing moves along quickly.

FOUNDATION BASICS

With the foundation method, an entire block is first drawn to scale on the chosen foundation material. The only seam allowance included is the one around the outer perimeter of the design. **Diagram 4** illustrates a typical template for the foundation method.

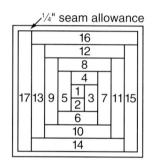

Diagram 4

The foundation technique used in this book involves positioning the fabric on one side of the foundation (the reverse side) and sewing on the opposite side (the front, marked side). Seams are stitched directly onto one of the marked lines of the template. If you are unfamiliar with this technique, it may at first seem awkward. But if you position the fabric correctly and are careful to sew on the lines, every log will be perfect, no matter how narrow its finished width.

Some quilters choose to piece on the front of a foundation, but that method requires that you use exact seam allowances. One advantage to choosing foundation piecing in the first place is its simplicity and speed, so it seems awkward to slow the process down by including a step that requires more precision.

There is one thing you must keep in mind as you work: Since the fabric will be sewn to the back of the foundation, the finished block will always be a *mirror image* of the template. For some blocks, such as those in the Pineapple Log Cabin quilt on page 22, this does not create a problem—the red and white areas are clearly defined. For others, getting the fabrics in the right place can sometimes be confusing. Where color or value may change from block to block, or where blocks are not symmetrical, misplaced fabric can alter your entire design.

It may be helpful to premark all or part of the logs of your foundation, on either the front or back side, as shown in **Diagram 5**. Jotting down simple designations such as light, dark, or the actual color of a log will save time and keep frustrating seam-ripping sessions to a minimum.

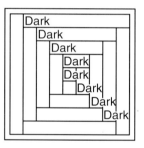

Diagram 5

FOUNDATION MATERIALS

There are two types of foundations—permanent and removable—and both are exactly what their names imply. Several types of materials fall into each category, all with advantages and disadvantages. Though the following list is by no means exhaustive, the descriptions may help you decide which type will be best for your project.

Permanent Foundations

Muslin is the most common example of a permanent foundation material. Some advantages include the following:

• The foundation will remain in the finished quilt permanently. The extra layer of fabric makes hand quilting more difficult, but since it adds more depth to the finished top, extensive quilting may not be necessary or desired. Many Log Cabin quilts with permanent foundations are tied rather than quilted.

• The extra fabric often eliminates the need for batting.

• The foundation will permanently stabilize the fabric, making careful placement of fabric grain less of a consideration.

• The foundation will help reinforce stitching, so seam allowances can be trimmed back a little more. This may help make outline quilting somewhat easier.

Some disadvantages of this type of foundation include:

• The material can stretch as it's handled. Be careful not to tug on the foundation too much as you work, or the block may become distorted. Tightly woven muslin will minimize the problem.

• The block sometimes seems to shrink as you add pieces. This is caused by the slight loft created by each new seam. The amount of shrinkage is usually very small, but should be considered if you plan to use a pieced border that must fit the quilt top exactly.

Two other options in the permanent foundation category include flannel and sheer interfacing. Flannel may be a bit harder to hold onto as you work, but it adds more depth and body than muslin. Spray-on starch or sizing will stiffen the flannel slightly, making it easier to handle. As for the interfacing, the additional layer it adds is easier to hand quilt through than muslin. Sheer interfacing is a good choice for those who intend to hand piece on a foundation.

Removable Foundations

Paper is the most commonly used removable foundation. Among its advantages are the following:

• The foundation will be removed after the top is assembled, and thus will not add an extra layer of fabric to your quilt.

• The paper will remain rigid as you work. There is no need to worry about distorting or shrinking the block.

• The cost of materials is very low.

Some of the disadvantages of paper as a foundation include:

• It can sometimes be time-consuming to remove, especially if pieces are very small.

• It will not remain in place to permanently stabilize the fabric, so cutting and positioning pieces on grain is more of a consideration.

Many types of paper can be used as foundation material. For example, blank newsprint is a good choice. It is sturdy enough to remain intact while handling, but pulls away easily when your top is complete. Newsprint is available in pads from 9 × 12 inches up to poster size, so it works well for blocks that are too large to draft onto a piece of 8½ × 11-inch paper.

Inexpensive copier paper, onion skin, and tracing papers are options for small blocks. Other foundation choices in the removable category include vanishing muslin, a loosely woven fabric that deteriorates and falls away when ironed, and tear-away paper, which is designed to be used as a stabilizer during machine embroidery.

TRANSFERRING THE IMAGE

There are several ways to transfer the template onto your foundation material.

Transfer Pens

Use a hot-iron transfer pen to draw the full-size block onto tracing paper. The image can usually be ironed onto a foundation material five or six times. Retrace over the original transfer for additional ironings, being careful to mark over the existing lines exactly. A transfer pen can be used on both fabric and paper foundations, but do a test first to be sure it will work on your chosen material.

Photocopies

Photocopies are an option for smaller blocks. The major disadvantage of photocopying is the slight distortion that's almost certain to occur. To minimize that distortion, make sure the page being copied is completely flat against the glass screen of the copier. Always check your copies to make sure blocks are square. Copiers can alter size slightly, too, so measure your copies carefully if a slight variation in block size will affect the finished quilt top. Always use the same generation of copies in your project, since copies of copies will usually be a slightly different size.

Computer Printouts

Those of you who use a computer to design quilt blocks can print the images directly onto paper. Most drawing programs have a "tile" feature that allows you to print large designs in segments, then tape the segments together to make a whole. For small blocks, some quilters feed freezer paper–backed muslin through their printers—but check with your printer's manufacturer before attempting that! In general, if a printer will accept card stock, it will probably process fabric. Printer ink should be tested for permanency on a piece of scrap fabric.

Light Box

A simple light box, or a lamp placed underneath a glass table, can be used to help you see the template clearly enough to trace it directly onto a foundation. However, with this method only one block can be drawn at a time. Blocks may be different due to slight tracing variations.

Other Considerations

Pens and other markers can be used to mark foundations. If you are using permanent foundations, be sure the markings on them are permanent, too, or that they will wash out completely without staining. You don't want your finished quilt to be ruined by bleeding ink during its first bath. Always check a new marker on scrap fabric before using it in a project, even if it's a brand you

have used before. If the ink bleeds, try to heat set it by ironing a marked scrap for a few minutes with a medium-hot iron. Check again for colorfastness. If the ink still bleeds, do not use it on permanent foundations.

Permanent inks are not necessary for removable foundations. Just be sure to choose a marking system that won't wear off onto fabric as you work.

FABRIC GRAIN

For maximum strength and stability and minimum distortion, fabric should be cut along its lengthwise or crosswise grain. Ideally, the straight of grain should be parallel with the outer perimeter of your block. For most pieces in Log Cabin quilts, this means positioning the grain line parallel to the seam. The rectangles, squares, and occasional triangles used to assemble quilt blocks in this book are simple shapes that will be easy to cut on grain. Grain placement is most important if you are using removable foundations that won't remain in the quilt as permanent stabilizers.

STITCH LENGTH

Most foundation piecing is done with a slightly shorter than normal stitch length. Twelve to 14 stitches per inch will produce good results. Be sure not to make your stitches too small, or they could cause unnecessary wear to the fabric. Also, very small stitches will be more difficult to remove if an error occurs.

Smaller stitches will "punch" your paper foundations, making them easier to remove. And smaller stitches are less likely to be distorted when foundations are pulled away.

PIECING A BLOCK

This section takes you step by step through the construction of one block. The block used as a sample is the block from the Nineteenth-Century Amish Log Cabin project, which begins on page 34. You may want to make a sample block here to learn the technique, or you may decide to select a project and jump right in. Even if you don't make a sample block, it's a good idea to read through all of the steps in this section so that you understand the process thoroughly before beginning any of the projects.

All of the foundation piecing instructions in this book contain recommended sizes for strip widths. It's easiest to cut long strips of fabric, then trim the logs to length as the block is assembled.

The strip width is based on the finished size of the log. The finished width of each log in this sample block is ¼ inch. If we add ¼ inch to each side to allow for seam allowances, the cut size becomes ¾ inch. When you first learn to piece on a foundation, it's usually best to add an additional ⅛ to ¼ inch to the calculated size. The extra bit of fabric will give you more flexibility as you position your strips onto the back of the foundation, and the excess will be trimmed away after sewing.

The Cutting Chart in each project takes this into consideration, calling for wider than necessary strips. However, since it will only take a practice block or two for you to become a foundation piecing pro, you may not want to cut extra-wide strips for the entire quilt. Cut just enough to construct one or two blocks to start with, then reevaluate the strip width, reducing it when you feel comfortable doing so. Never cut the strips narrower than the finished width plus ¼-inch seam allowance on each side.

For the sample block, make a foundation from the pattern on page 42. Start by cutting ⅞-inch- to 1-inch-wide strips across the width of your fabrics. Since the extra width will be trimmed away after sewing, the method may at first seem wasteful, but remember that you'll probably decrease the width after one or two blocks. Even if you prefer to continue using wider than necessary strips, the time you'll save and the perfect results you'll achieve by piecing on a foundation will likely make the use of additional fabric an unimportant consideration.

Step 1. Pieces are sewn to the foundation in numerical order. Cut a ¾-inch square from the fabric you set aside for the center piece, log 1. Place it right side up on the back side of your foundation, centering it over the lines surrounding the area for log 1, as shown in **Diagram 6**. Use tape, a dab of glue stick, or a pin to hold the fabric in place.

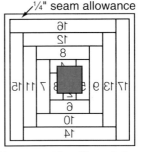

Reverse side of foundation

Diagram 6

Step 2. Hold the foundation up to the light with the back side away from you. You should be able to see the shadow of log 1. Does the shadow overlap all drawn lines for log 1? Is the overlap sufficient to create a stable seam allowance when those lines are sewn? If not, reposition the piece and check again before continuing.

Step 3. Find the strip of fabric set aside for log 2 and position it on the back side of your foundation, right side down. Align the strip along the left and lower edges of log 1, as shown in **Diagram 7A**. The strip will entirely cover log 1.

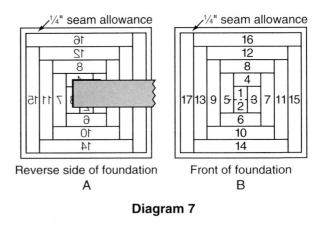

Reverse side of foundation   Front of foundation
A   B

Diagram 7

Step 4. Holding the strip in place, flip the foundation over. Sew on the line separating log 1 from log 2, beginning and ending approximately

⅛ inch on either side of the line, as shown in **7B** on page 125. Remove the foundation from the machine.

Step 5. Flip again to the back side of your foundation. Trim away the excess tail of fabric from log 2 just past the end of the seam line, as shown in **Diagram 8A.** If necessary, trim away excess fabric from the seam allowance you've created. If you used tape to secure the first piece, remove it now.

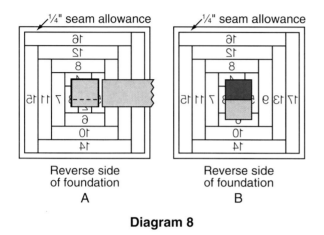

Diagram 8

Step 6. Flip log 2 into a right-side-up position, finger pressing it firmly into place. If you prefer, keep an iron near your work area to press pieces as you go. The back side of your foundation should now resemble **8B.**

Step 7. Hold the foundation up to the light with the back side away from you. You will now be able to see the shadow created by the fabric for log 2. Its raw edges should overlap all unsewn seam lines for log 2. This assures you there will be sufficient seam allowance on all sides when you add the adjacent logs.

One way to judge whether your strip has been placed correctly is to take a look at your seam allowance before trimming away the excess. Is it overly wide? If so, the piece you've just sewn may have been positioned incorrectly on the foundation. **Diagram 9** shows two examples of log 2 placement; here log 2 appears transparent to make the differences easier to see. In **9A,** the strip is aligned against the left and lower edges of log 1, as

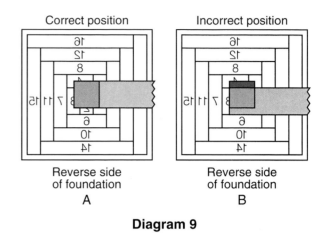

Diagram 9

directed in Step 3. In **9B,** the strip is aligned lower on log 1.

When the seam in **9B** is stitched, it will have a larger than necessary seam allowance, stealing width from the log 2 fabric. The remaining width may not be adequate to cover the area for log 2 and create a stable seam allowance on its remaining sides when the fabric is flipped into place. **Diagram 10** illustrates the result: This strip is now too narrow to have an adequate seam along its lower edge.

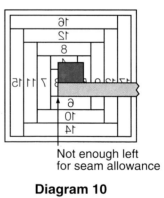

Diagram 10

Step 8. Log 3 is added in exactly the same way as log 2. Position a strip of fabric right side down on the foundation, aligning its top with log 1 and its left edge with the left edges of logs 1 and 2, as shown in **Diagram 11A.** The strip will completely cover the sewn pieces.

Flip the foundation over, and sew on the vertical line separating log 3 from logs 1 and 2, beginning and ending approximately ⅛ inch on either side of the line. Remove the foundation from the machine.

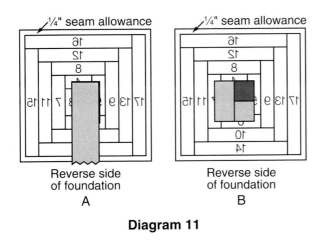

Reverse side
of foundation
A

Reverse side
of foundation
B

Diagram 11

Step 9. Trim the excess tail from log 3. Trim excess seam allowance if necessary. Flip log 3 into a right-side-up position, finger pressing it firmly into place. The reverse side of your foundation should now resemble **11B**.

Step 10. Position log 4 right side down on the foundation, as shown in **Diagram 12A**. Holding the fabric in place, flip the foundation over and sew on the horizontal line separating log 4 from logs 1 and 3. Remember to begin and end the seam approximately ⅛ inch on either side of the line. Remove the foundation from the machine.

Step 11. Turn the foundation over to the back side, and trim the excess tail of fabric from log 4,

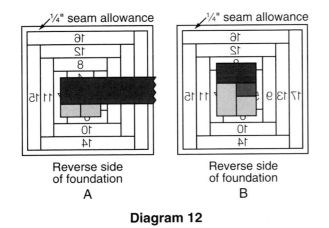

Reverse side
of foundation
A

Reverse side
of foundation
B

Diagram 12

just as you did with the previous logs. Trim excess seam allowance if necessary, then finger press log 4 into a right-side-up position. The back side of your foundation should now resemble **12B**.

Step 12. Sew all remaining logs to the foundation in exactly the same way. After adding log 7, the back of your foundation should resemble **Diagram 13A** and the front side should resemble **13B**. Notice that each new seam acts as a stabilizer for those it intersects.

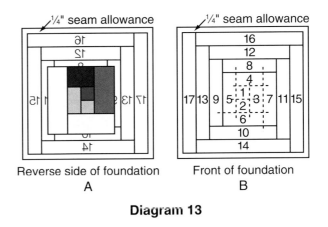

Reverse side of foundation
A

Front of foundation
B

Diagram 13

Step 13. Log 17 is the final piece for this block. After it has been added, press the entire block lightly. Align your plastic ruler with an *outer* line of the seam allowance, and cut directly on the line with your rotary cutter. Be careful not to cut off the seam allowance. Repeat for the remaining outer lines. Leave removable foundations in place until your quilt top is assembled.

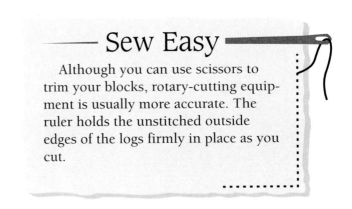

Sew Easy

Although you can use scissors to trim your blocks, rotary-cutting equipment is usually more accurate. The ruler holds the unstitched outside edges of the logs firmly in place as you cut.

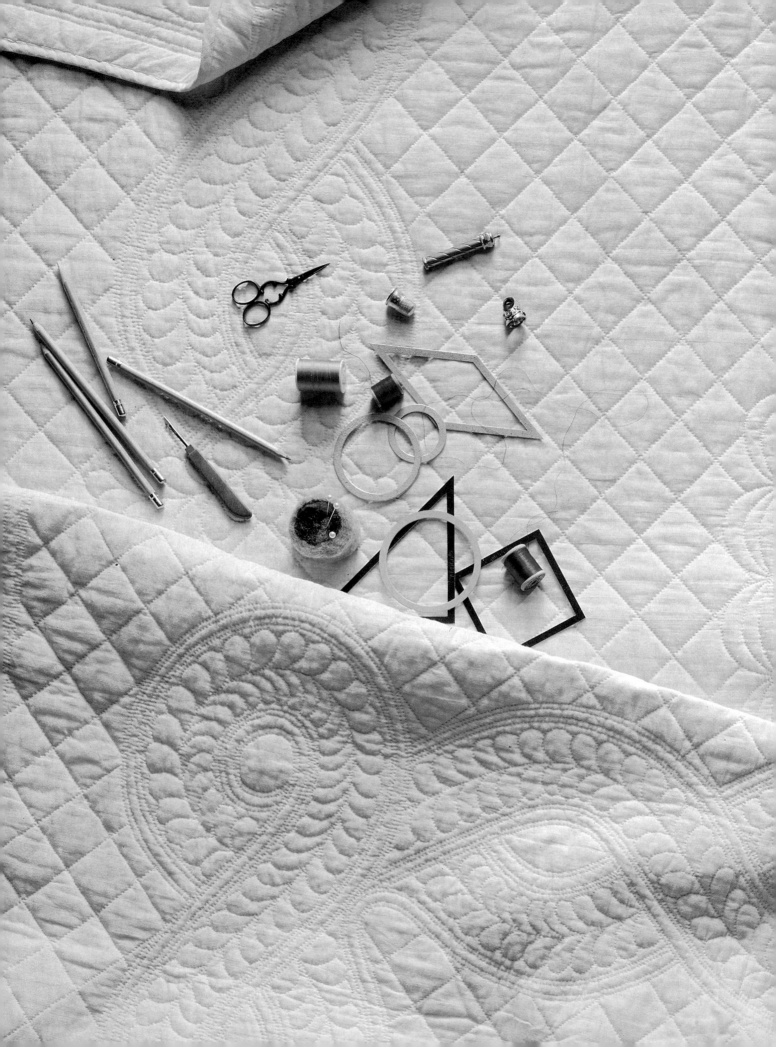

QUILTMAKING
BASICS

This section provides a refresher course in basic quiltmaking techniques. Refer to it as needed; it will help not only with the projects in this book but also with all your quiltmaking.

QUILTMAKER'S BASIC SUPPLY LIST

Here's a list of items you should have on hand before beginning a project.

• **Iron and ironing board:** Make sure these are set up near your sewing machine. Careful pressing leads to accurate piecing.

• **Needles:** The two types of needles commonly used by quilters are *betweens,* short needles used for quilting, and *sharps,* long, very thin needles used for appliqué and hand piecing. The thickness of hand-sewing needles decreases as their size designation increases. For instance, a size 12 needle is smaller than a size 10.

• **Rotary cutter, plastic ruler, and cutting mat:** Fabric can be cut quickly and accurately with rotary-cutting equipment. There are a variety of cutters available, all with slightly different handle styles and safety latches. Rigid, see-through plastic rulers are used with rotary cutters. A 6 × 24-inch ruler is a good size; for the most versatility, be sure it has 45 degree and 60 degree angle markings. A 14-inch square ruler will also be helpful for making sure blocks are square. Always use a special mat with a rotary cutter. The mat protects the work surface and helps to grip the fabric. Purchase the largest mat practical for your sewing area. A good all-purpose size is 18 × 24 inches.

• **Safety pins:** These are generally used to baste quilts for machine quilting. Use rustproof nickel-plated brass safety pins, preferably in size #0.

• **Scissors:** You'll need several pairs of scissors—shears for cutting fabric, general scissors for cutting paper and template plastic, and small, sharp embroidery scissors for trimming threads.

• **Seam ripper:** A seam ripper with a small, extra-fine blade slips easily under any stitch length.

• **Sewing machine:** Any machine with a straight stitch is suitable for piecing quilt blocks. Follow the manufacturer's recommendations for cleaning and servicing your sewing machine.

• **Straight pins:** Choose long, thin pins with glass or plastic heads that are easy to see against fabric so that you don't forget to remove one.

• **Template material:** Sheets of clear and opaque template plastic can be purchased at most quilt or craft shops. Gridded plastic is also available and may help you to draw shapes more easily. Various weights of cardboard can also be used for templates, including common household items like cereal boxes, poster board, and manila file folders.

• **Thimbles:** For hand quilting, a thimble is almost essential. Look for one that fits the finger you use to push the needle. The thimble should be snug enough to stay put when you shake your hand. There should be a bit of space between the end of your finger and the inside of the thimble.

• **Thread:** For hand or machine piecing, 100 percent cotton thread is a traditional favorite. Cotton-covered polyester is also acceptable. For hand quilting, use 100 percent cotton quilting thread. For machine quilting, you may want to try clear nylon thread as the top thread, with cotton thread in the bobbin.

• **Tweezers:** Keep a pair of tweezers handy for removing bits of thread from ripped-out seams and for pulling away scraps of removable foundations. Regular cosmetic tweezers will work fine.

SELECTING AND PREPARING FABRICS

The traditional fabric choice for quilts is 100 percent cotton. It handles well, is easy to care for, presses easily, and frays less than synthetic blends.

The yardages in this book are generous estimates based on 44/45-inch-wide fabrics. It's a good idea to always purchase a bit more fabric than necessary to compensate for shrinkage and occasional cutting errors.

Prewash your fabrics using warm water and a mild soap or detergent. Test for colorfastness by first soaking a scrap in warm water. If colors bleed, set the dye by soaking the whole piece of fabric in a solution of 3 parts cold water to 1 part vinegar. Rinse the fabric several times in warm water. If it still bleeds, don't use it in a quilt that will need laundering—save it for a wallhanging that won't get a lot of use.

After washing, preshrink your fabric by drying it in a dryer on the medium setting. To keep wrinkles under control, remove the fabric from the dryer while it's still slightly damp and press it immediately with a hot iron.

CUTTING FABRIC

The cutting instructions for each project follow the list of materials. Whenever possible, the instructions are written to take advantage of quick rotary-cutting techniques. In addition, some projects include patterns for those who prefer to make templates and scissor cut individual pieces.

Although rotary cutting can be faster and more accurate than scissor cutting, it has one disadvantage: It does not always result in the most efficient use of fabric. In some cases, the method results in long strips of leftover fabric. Don't think of these as waste; just add them to your scrap bag for future projects.

Rotary-Cutting Basics

Follow these two safety rules every time you use a rotary cutter: Always cut *away* from yourself, and always slide the blade guard into place as soon as you stop cutting.

Step 1: You can cut several layers of fabric at a time with a rotary cutter. Fold the fabric with the selvage edges together. You can fold it again if you want, doubling the number of layers to be cut.

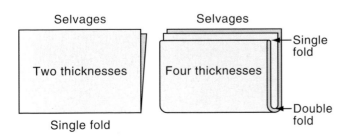

Step 2: To square up the end of the fabric, place a ruled square on the fold and slide a 6 × 24-inch ruler against the side of the square. Hold the ruler in place, remove the square, and cut along the edge of the ruler. If you are left-handed, work from the other end of the fabric.

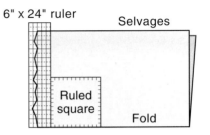

Step 3: For patchwork, cut strips or rectangles on the crosswise grain, then subcut them into smaller pieces as needed. The diagram shows a strip cut into squares.

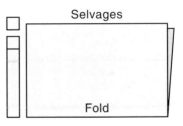

Step 4: A square can be subcut into two triangles by making one diagonal cut (A). Two diagonal cuts yield four triangles (B).

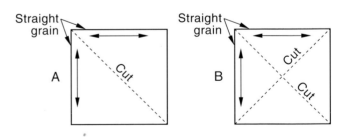

Step 5: Check strips periodically to make sure they're straight and not angled. If they are angled, refold the fabric and square up the edges again.

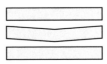

ENLARGING PATTERNS

Every effort has been made to provide full-size pattern pieces. But in some cases, where the pattern piece is too large to fit on the page, the pattern runs at a reduced size. Instructions below the pattern will tell you how much it needs to be enlarged to make it full size. Take the book to a photocopier and enlarge by the percentage indicated on the pattern.

MAKING AND USING TEMPLATES

To make a plastic template, place template plastic over the book page, trace the pattern onto the plastic, and cut out the template. To make a cardboard template, copy the pattern onto tracing paper, glue the paper to the cardboard, and cut out the template. With a permanent marker, record on every template any identification letters and grain lines, as well as the size and name of the block and the number of pieces needed. Always check your templates against the printed pattern for accuracy.

The patchwork patterns in this book are printed with double lines. The inner dashed line is the finished size of the piece, while the outer solid line includes seam allowance.

For hand piecing: Trace the inner line to make finished-size templates. Cut out the templates on the traced line. Draw around the templates on the wrong side of the fabric, leaving ½ inch between pieces. Then mark ¼-inch seam allowances before you cut out the pieces.

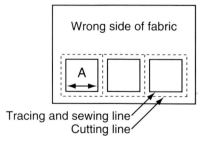

Wrong side of fabric

A

Tracing and sewing line
Cutting line

For machine piecing: Trace the outer solid line on the printed pattern to make templates with seam allowance included. Draw around the templates on the wrong side of the fabric and cut out the pieces on this line.

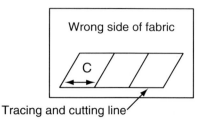

Wrong side of fabric

C

Tracing and cutting line

For appliqué: Appliqué patterns in this book have only a single line and are finished size. Draw around the templates on the right side of the fabric, leaving ½ inch between pieces. Add ⅛- to ¼-inch seam allowances by eye as you cut the pieces.

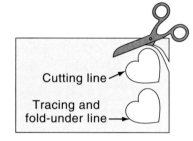

Cutting line

Tracing and
fold-under line

PIECING BASICS

Standard seam allowance for piecing is ¼ inch. Machine sew a sample seam to test the accuracy of the seam allowance; adjust as needed. For hand piecing, the sewing line is marked on the fabric.

Hand Piecing

Cut fabric pieces using finished-size templates. Place the pieces right sides together, match marked seam lines, and pin. Use a running stitch along the marked line, backstitching every four or five stitches and at the beginning and end of the seam.

When you cross seam allowances of previously joined units, leave the seam allowances free. Backstitch just before you cross, slip the needle through the seam allowance, backstitch just after you cross, then resume stitching the seam.

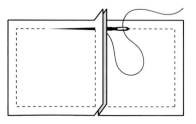

Machine Piecing

Cut the fabric pieces using templates with seam allowances included or using a rotary cutter and ruler without templates. Set the stitch length at 10 to 12 stitches per inch.

Place the fabric pieces right sides together, then sew from raw edge to raw edge. Press seams before crossing them with other seams, pressing toward the darker fabric whenever possible.

Chain piecing: Use this technique when you need to sew more than one of the same type of unit. Place the fabric pieces right sides together and, without lifting the presser foot or cutting the thread, run the pairs through the sewing machine one after another. Once all the units you need have been sewn, snip them apart and press.

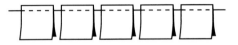

Setting In Pieces

Pattern pieces must sometimes be set into angles created by other pieces, as shown in the diagram. Here, pieces A, B, and C are set into the angles created by the four joined diamond pieces.

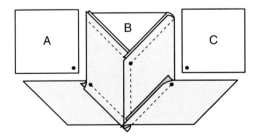

Step 1: Keep the seam allowances open where the piece is to be set in. Begin by sewing the first seam in the usual manner, beginning and ending the seam ¼ inch from the edge of the fabric and backstitching at each end.

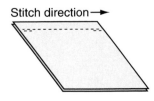

Step 2: Open up the pattern pieces and place the piece to be set in right sides together with one of the first two pieces. Begin the seam ¼ inch from the edge of the fabric and sew to the exact point where the first seam ended, backstitching at the beginning and end of the seam.

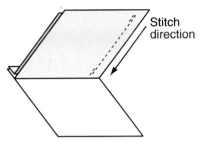

Step 3: Rotate the pattern pieces so that you are ready to sew the final seam. Keeping the seam allowances free, sew from the point where the last seam ended to ¼ inch from the edge of the piece.

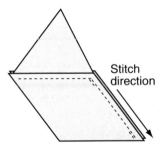

Step 4: Press the seams so that as many of them as possible lie flat. The finished unit should look like the one shown here.

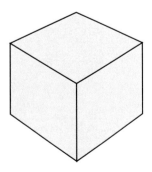

APPLIQUÉ BASICS

Review "Making and Using Templates" to learn how to prepare templates for appliqué. Lightly draw around each template on the right side of the fabric using a pencil or other nonpermanent marker. These are the fold-under lines. Cut out the pieces ⅛ to ¼ inch to the outside of the marked lines.

The Needle-Turn Method

Pin the pieces in position on the background fabric, always working in order from the background to the foreground. For best results, don't turn under or appliqué edges that will be covered by other appliqué pieces. Use a thread color that matches the fabric of the appliqué piece.

Step 1: Bring the needle up from under the appliqué patch exactly on the drawn line. Fold under the seam allowance on the line to neatly encase the knot.

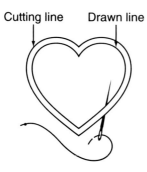

Cutting line   Drawn line

Step 2: Insert the tip of the needle into the background fabric right next to where the thread comes out of the appliqué piece. Bring the needle out of the background fabric approximately ¹⁄₁₆ inch away from and up through the very edge of the fold, completing the first stitch.

Step 3: Repeat this process for each stitch, using the tip and shank of your appliqué needle to turn under ½-inch-long sections of seam allowance at a time. As you turn under a section, press it flat with your thumb and then stitch it in place, as shown.

PRESSING BASICS

Proper pressing can make a big difference in the appearance of a finished block or quilt top. It allows patchwork to open up to its full size, permits more precise matching of seams, and results in smooth, flat work. Quilters are divided on the issue of whether a steam or dry iron is best; experiment to see which works best for you. Keep these tips in mind:

• Press seam allowances to one side, not open. Whenever possible, press toward the darker fabric. If you find you must press toward a lighter fabric, trim the dark seam allowance slightly to prevent show-through.

• Press seams of adjacent rows of blocks, or rows within blocks, in opposite directions. The pressed seams will fit together snugly, producing precise intersections.

• Press, don't iron. Bring the iron down gently and firmly. This is especially important if you are using steam.

• To press appliqués, lay a towel on the ironing board, turn the piece right side down on the towel, and press very gently on the back side.

ASSEMBLING QUILT TOPS

Lay out all the blocks for your quilt top using the quilt diagram or photo as a guide to placement. Pin and sew the blocks together in vertical or horizontal rows for straight-set quilts and in diagonal rows for diagonal-set quilts. Press the seam allowances in opposite directions from row to row so that the seams will fit together snugly when rows are joined.

To keep a large quilt top manageable, join rows into pairs first and then join the pairs. When pressing a completed quilt top, press on the back side first, carefully clipping and removing hanging threads; then press the front.

MITERING BORDERS

Step 1: Start by measuring the length of your finished quilt top through the center. Add to that figure two times the width of the border, plus 5 inches extra. This is the length you need to cut the two side borders. For example, if the quilt top is 48 inches long and the border is 4 inches wide, you need two borders that are each 61 inches long (48 + 4 + 4 + 5 = 61). In the same manner, calculate the length of the top and bottom borders, then cut the borders.

Step 2: Sew each of the borders to the quilt top, beginning and ending the seams ¼ inch from the edge of the quilt. Press the border seams flat from the right side of the quilt.

Step 3: Working at one corner of the quilt, place one border on top of the adjacent border. Fold the top border under so that it meets the edge of the other border and forms a 45 degree angle, as shown in the diagram. If you are working with a plaid or striped border, check to make sure the stripes match along this folded edge. Press the fold in place.

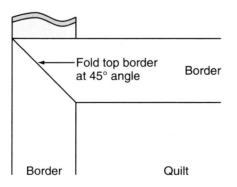

Step 4: Fold the quilt top with right sides together and align the edges of the borders. With the pressed fold as the corner seam line and the

body of the quilt out of the way, sew from the inner corner to the outer corner, as shown in the diagram.

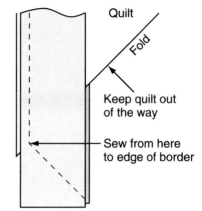

Step 5: Unfold the quilt and check to make sure that all points match and the miter is flat. Trim the border seam allowance to ¼ inch and press the seam open.

Step 6: Repeat Steps 3 through 5 for the three remaining borders.

MARKING QUILTING DESIGNS

To mark a quilting design, use a commercially made stencil, make your own stencil using a sheet of plastic, or trace the design from a book page. Use a nonpermanent marker, such as a silver or white pencil, chalk pencil, or chalk marker, that will be visible on the fabric. You can even mark with a 0.5 mm lead pencil, but be sure to mark lightly.

If you are using a quilt design from this book, either trace the design onto tracing paper or photocopy it. If the pattern will be used many times, glue it to cardboard to make it sturdy.

For light-color fabrics that you can see through, place the pattern under the quilt top and trace the quilting design directly onto the fabric. Mark in a thin, continuous line that will be covered by the quilting thread.

With dark fabrics, mark from the top by drawing around a hard-edged design template. To make a simple template, trace the design onto template plastic and cut it out around the outer edge. Trace around the template onto the fabric, then add inner lines by eye.

LAYERING AND BASTING

Carefully preparing the quilt top, batting, and backing will ensure that the finished quilt will lie flat and smooth. Place the backing wrong side up on a large table or clean floor. Center the batting on the backing and smooth out any wrinkles. Center the quilt top right side up on the batting; smooth it out and remove any loose threads.

If you plan to hand quilt, baste the quilt with thread. Use a long darning needle and white thread. Baste outward from the center of the quilt in a grid of horizontal and vertical rows approximately 4 inches apart.

If you plan to machine quilt, baste with safety pins. Thread basting does not hold the layers securely enough during machine quilting, plus the thread is more difficult to remove when quilting is completed. Use rustproof nickel-plated brass safety pins in size #0, pinning from the center of the quilt out approximately every 3 inches.

HAND QUILTING

For best results, use a hoop or a frame to hold the quilt layers taut and smooth during quilting. Work with one hand on top of the quilt and the other hand underneath, guiding the needle. Don't worry about the size of your stitches in the beginning; concentrate on making them even, and they will get smaller over time.

Getting started: Thread a needle with quilting thread and knot the end. Insert the needle through the quilt top and batting about 1 inch away from where you will begin stitching. Bring the needle to the surface in position to make the first stitch. Gently tug on the thread to pop the knot through the quilt top and bury it in the batting.

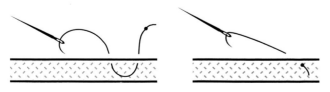

Taking the stitches: Insert the needle through the three layers of the quilt. When you feel the tip of the needle with your underneath finger, gently guide it back up through the quilt. When the needle comes through the top of the quilt, press your thimble on the end with the eye to guide it down again through the quilt layers. Continue to quilt in this manner, taking two or three small running stitches at a time.

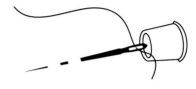

Ending a line of stitching: Bring the needle to the top of the quilt just past the last stitch. Make a knot at the surface by bringing the needle under the thread where it comes out of the fabric and up through the loop of thread it creates. Repeat this knot and insert the needle into the hole where the thread comes out of the fabric. Run the needle inside the batting for an inch and bring it back to the surface. Tug gently on the thread to pop the knot into the batting layer. Clip the thread.

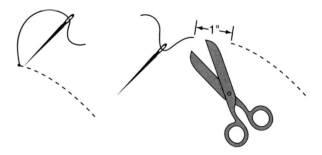

MACHINE QUILTING

For best results when doing machine-guided quilting, use a walking foot (also called an even feed foot) on your sewing machine. For free-motion quilting, use a darning or machine-embroidery foot.

Use thread to match the fabric colors, or use clear nylon thread in the top of the machine and a white or colored thread in the bobbin. To secure the thread at the beginning of a line of stitches, adjust the stitch length on your machine to make several very short stitches, then gradually increase to the regular stitch length. As you near the end of the line, gradually reduce the stitch length so that the last few stitches are very short.

For machine-guided quilting, keep the feed dogs up and move all three layers as smoothly as you can under the needle. To turn a corner in a quilting design, stop with the needle inserted in the fabric, raise the foot, pivot the quilt, lower the foot, and continue stitching.

For free-motion quilting, disengage the feed dogs so you can manipulate the quilt freely as you stitch. Guide the quilt under the needle with both hands, coordinating the speed of the needle with the movement of the quilt to create stitches of consistent length.

MAKING AND ATTACHING BINDING

Double-fold binding, which is also called French-fold binding, can be made from either straight-grain or bias strips. To make double-fold binding, cut strips of fabric four times the finished width of the binding, plus seam allowance. In general, cut strips 2 inches wide for quilts with thin batting and 2¼ inches wide for quilts with thicker batting.

Making Straight-Grain Binding

To make straight-grain binding, cut crosswise strips from the binding fabric in the desired width. Sew them together end to end with diagonal seams.

Place the strips with right sides together so that each strip is set in ¼ inch from the end of the other strip. Sew a diagonal seam and trim the excess fabric, leaving a ¼-inch seam allowance.

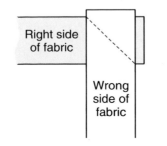

Making Continuous Bias Binding

Bias binding can be cut in one long strip from a square of fabric that has been cut apart and resewn into a tube. To estimate the number of inches of binding a particular square will produce, use this formula:

Multiply the length of one side by the length of another side, and divide the result by the width of binding you want. Using a 30-inch square and 2¼-inch binding as an example: $30 \times 30 = 900 \div 2\frac{1}{4} = 400$ inches of binding.

Step 1: To make bias binding, cut a square in half diagonally to get two triangles. Place the two triangles right sides together as shown and sew with a ¼-inch seam. Open out the two pieces and press the seam open.

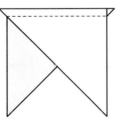

Step 2: Mark cutting lines on the wrong side of the fabric in the desired binding width. Mark the lines parallel to the bias edges.

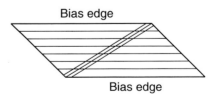

Step 3: Fold the fabric with right sides together, bringing the two nonbias edges together and offsetting them by one strip width (shown at the top of page 138). Pin the edges together, creating a tube, and sew with a ¼-inch seam. Press the seam open.

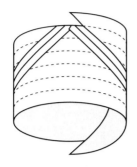

Step 4: Cut on the marked lines, turning the tube to cut one long bias strip.

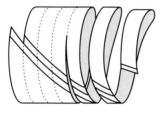

Attaching the Binding

Trim excess batting and backing even with the quilt top. For double-fold binding, fold the long binding strip in half lengthwise, wrong sides together, and press. Beginning in the middle of a side, not in a corner, place the strip right sides together with the quilt top, align the raw edges, and pin.

Step 1: Fold over approximately 1 inch at the beginning of the strip and begin stitching ½ inch from the fold. Sew the binding to the quilt, using a ¼-inch seam and stitching through all layers.

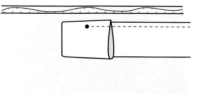

Step 2: As you approach a corner, stop stitching ¼ inch from the raw edge of the corner. Backstitch and remove the quilt from the machine. Fold the binding strip up at a 45 degree angle, as shown in the following diagram on the left. Fold the strip back down so there is a fold at the upper

edge, as shown on the right. Begin sewing at the top edge of the quilt, continuing to the next corner. Miter all four corners in this manner.

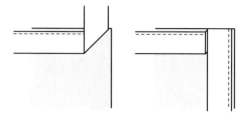

Step 3: To finish the binding seam, overlap the folded-back beginning section with the ending section. Stitch across the fold, allowing the end to extend approximately ½ inch beyond the beginning.

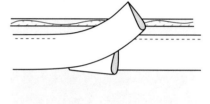

Step 4: Turn the binding to the back of the quilt and blindstitch the folded edge in place, covering the machine stitches with the folded edge. Fold in the adjacent sides on the back and take several stitches in the miter. In the same way, add several stitches to the miters on the front.

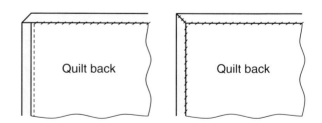

SIGNING YOUR QUILT

Be sure to sign and date your finished quilt. Your finishing touch can be a simple signature in permanent ink or an elaborate inked or embroidered label. Add any other pertinent details that can help family members or quilt collectors 100 years from now understand what went into your labor of love.